STEP BY STEP TO GRACE

STEP BY STEP TO GRACE

A Spiritual Walk
Through the Bible
and the Twelve Steps

Lorraine Milton

NOVALIS

© 2002 Novalis, Saint Paul University, Ottawa, Canada

Cover design and layout: Caroline Gagnon
Cover photograph: Eyewire

Business Office:
Novalis
49 Front Street East, 2nd Floor
Toronto, Ontario, Canada
M5E 1B3

Phone: 1-800-387-7164 or (416) 363-3303
Fax: 1-800-204-4140 or (416) 363-9409
E-mail: cservice@novalis.ca

A catalogue record for this book is available from the National Library of Canada.
ISBN 2-89507-277-9
C2002-902971-6

Printed in Canada.

Unless otherwise noted, the Scripture quotations contained herein are from the
New Revised Standard Version of the Bible, copyrighted 1989 by the Division of
Christian Education of the National Council of the Churches of Christ in the
United States of America, and are used by permission. All rights reserved.

The Twelve Steps and excerpts from the book, *Alcoholics Anonymous* are
reprinted with permission of Alcoholics Anonymous World Services, Inc.
(A.A.W.S.) Permission to reprint the Twelve Steps and excerpts from
Alcoholics Anonymous does not mean that A.A.W.S. has reviewed or approved
the contents of this publication, or that A.A.W.S. necessarily agrees with the
views expressed herein. A.A. is a program of recovery from alcoholism only –
use of the Twelve Steps in connection with programs and activities which are
patterned after A.A., but which address other problems, or in any other non-
A.A. context, does not imply otherwise. Although Alcoholics Anonymous is a
spiritual program, A.A. is not a religious program, and use of A.A. material in
the present connection does not imply A.A.'s affiliation with or endorsement
of, any sect, denomination, or specific religious belief.

We acknowledge the financial support of the Government of Canada through
the Book Publishing Industry Development Program (BPIDP) for our
publishing activities.

10 9 8 7 6 5 4 3 2 1   10 09 08 07 06 05 04 03 02

*In memory of
my mother and father,
Ida and Frank Sisco*

Commit your work to the Lord,
and your plans will be established.

Proverbs 16:3

Contents

Preface

For eight years, I worked as a chaplain in the area of addictions, and I heard many sad stories. Women have spoken to me again and again of their pain and rage and their sense of rejection. Out of this collective suffering, this book was born.

Through my own life experiences and through listening to others, I have come to believe that a rock bottom or crisis situation can be an opportunity or turning point for change. It is often during the worst times of our lives that we come to the realization that we are spiritually, emotionally and physically bankrupt. It is only then that we are ready to ask for divine assistance. It is only then that we choose to depend on God and take that first step on the road to recovery.

When women are hurt – by people or institutions – they suffer in their relationships with self and others. Many have told me that because of the physical, psychological and spiritual abuse that has been inflicted upon them in the name of Christianity, they have simply given up on God. As a result of their hurt and disillusionment, addictions have become an antidote – an attempt to dull the pain.

Step by Step to Grace offers hope and comfort to women who are struggling with various forms of addiction and dysfunctional behaviour. Based on the principles of the Bible and Alcoholics Anonymous (AA), this book explores women's key issues of relationships, self-worth, sexuality and spirituality.

Let me help you to read the Bible with new eyes, so that it can become a source of support and encouragement throughout your recovery process. Through an exploration of AA's Twelve Steps, I will show you how to do the honest work necessary for self-discovery, self-care and personal growth. It is my hope that this book will reassure you that God will never betray your trust.

In *Part One: Recovery*, each step begins with a passage from the Bible. The discussion that follows includes anecdotes, the expertise of other writers, and my own insights and observations. As well as detailing the struggles of recovery, this section offers guidance within a Christian context and invites you to live "fully" as you embrace the principles and apply them to your everyday life. For your efforts, you will be blessed with the strength and courage you need to persevere.

Part Two: Words of Consolation consists of biblical quotations and inspirational writings relevant to each step. You can use these quotations, as well as others that are interspersed throughout Part One, for meditation purposes. The Bibliography provides ample ideas for further study.

As you explore this book, you will meet other women who have suffered. (Names have been changed and, at times, experiences have been combined to protect the identity of individuals.) You will also find ways to move beyond your pain. With God's help, you will receive true healing and the gift of grace.

Although this book is primarily focused on women in recovery and those still struggling with addiction, I believe it can appeal to all women dealing with shame, low self-esteem and feelings of powerlessness. Place your trust in God, and find your way to grace, step by step.

Part One

Recovery

Introduction

Recovery is about rebuilding and reclaiming our spiritual heritage as children of God. It is about being willing to change destructive attitudes and behaviours and allowing God to heal our broken humanity. Whenever we displace God for the idols of addiction, the results are isolation, devastation and eventual despair. Recovery is about saying "no" to this oppression and "yes" to the celebration of life – and to a radically new lifestyle. As Jesus said: "I came that they may have life, and have it abundantly." (John 10:10) This is the good news that quenches our spiritual thirst and liberates us from the bondage and paralysis of our addictions, good news that renews our faith, restores our dignity and supports our lives "abundantly."

Both the Bible and the guidelines of Alcoholics Anonymous – the Big Book – contain principles that help us to find and maintain spiritual, emotional, mental and physical well-being in our daily lives. These principles enable us to reconnect with our positive spiritual energy, energy that we have blocked and aborted through addiction.

Many of us have become distrustful of anything religious. Distorted and rigid views, perhaps gleaned from childhood or our faith traditions, may have left us embittered. Thus, we may discount the Bible and the Twelve Steps, unable to recognize them as spiritual resources that can bring about a new relationship with God, our neighbours and ourselves.

Many women find the Bible's patriarchal overtones, subordination of women and non-inclusive language offensive, demeaning and even detrimental to their welfare. We must remember, however, that the gospel writers wrote from a cultural context that reflected the faith journey of their male-dominated society. The gospels were written long ago and translated from the male perspective in a society that devalued women and anything feminine. This misogyny is vividly portrayed in the story of Lot offering his two virgin daughters as sacrifices to appease a mob that threatened two male guests in his house (Genesis 19:8). Evidently, this behaviour was socially acceptable at the time.

The Hebrew-Jewish lifestyle depicted in the Bible and presented as sacred has been used for centuries to reinforce the inferiority of women in society and culture. Fortunately, these attitudes and beliefs do not reflect the true spirit of Christianity. When we read the Bible with new eyes, we see that Jesus Christ never treated women as inferior. On the contrary, he powerfully defended their equality and humanity many times in his ministry.

In a culture where women were chattels, Jesus broke the rules of the day. His positive attitude is especially evident in the story of the Samaritan woman at the well

(John 4:4-42). In this story, Jesus behaves in a scandalous fashion, violating societal codes by conversing with a Samaritan (the Samaritans were a despised people). If that isn't bad enough, she is a woman and an outcast. Jesus ignores the Jewish prohibition against speaking to women in public, and accepts a drink from her despite the Jewish belief that all Samaritan women were unclean from birth. From their encounter something surprising happens: this Samaritan woman, a sinner and an outcast, reveals the news of the Messiah to her townspeople.

It was through the body of a woman – Mary – that Jesus came into the world (Luke 1:26-38). After his death on the cross, it was to Mary Magdalene and the other Mary that he first appeared, and they in turn bore witness to his resurrection (Matthew 28:9-10). These passages clearly show women as chosen disciples and bearers of good news.

Jesus' positive regard for women is again reflected in the Gospel of John (8:1-11), where the Pharisees had brought forth a woman caught in the act of adultery. At that time, the punishment for an adulteress was death by stoning, but Jesus spared her, saying, "Go your way, and from now on do not sin again."

Women were an important part of Jesus' ministry, and his relationship with them was based on principles of equality and inclusivity. He also challenged and discarded the ancient law that prohibited women from studying the Scriptures with a rabbi. These female scholars became courageous and loyal followers as they, too, had to break with tradition in order to go with Jesus. These acts show that Jesus' love and acceptance was extended to all, regardless of race, creed or gender.

The Old Testament documents the spiritual journey of the Israelites and their struggle to come to terms with the mystery of God and the meaning of life. They saw the LORD as a compassionate deity, the one who delivered them out of the bondage of Egypt and journeyed with them to the promised land. However, they also experienced him as a harsh, judgmental deity meting out cruel punishments for their transgressions.

Throughout the New Testament, however, Jesus constantly presents God as a loving and all-merciful parent. Through the presence of Jesus Christ, the Spirit of God is made manifest. This is a God who is involved with the poor, the homeless, the sick, the downtrodden and the outcast. This God is totally immersed in the welfare of humanity, and Jesus' actions are a visible sign of God's all-inclusive love – a love that transcends all the divisions fostered by racial, ethnic, social, gender or religious prejudices.

Jesus' compassion and concern for marginalized people was a radical concept for his day. Many of his acts were abhorrent to the Scribes and Pharisees, whose focus on the letter of the law dictated what was considered appropriate social and moral behaviour. Because their rules and regulations were often heartless and limiting, Jesus broke the rules repeatedly. He was condemned for healing the sick on the Sabbath because it broke the Sabbath law. His retort to the Pharisees was, "The Sabbath was made for humankind, and not humankind for the Sabbath; so the Son of Man is lord even of the Sabbath." (Mark 2:27-28)

Jesus felt free to interpret Scripture in a revolutionary fashion, as he did in the Sermon on the Mount when he stated: "Do not think that I have come to abolish the law or the prophets; I have come not to abolish but to fulfill…. For I tell you, unless your righteousness exceeds that of the Scribes and Pharisees, you will never enter the kingdom of heaven." He then issued new instructions about such issues as murder, anger, adultery, divorce, oaths, retaliation, enemies, almsgiving, prayer, fasting and treasures (Matthew 5:17-48 – 6:1-21).

Jesus was telling his listeners that external rules alone are not enough to grant them entry into the kingdom of heaven. Spiritual nourishment must come from within, through the internal codes of love, compassion and respect for all humankind, which imprint themselves upon the heart. The rules must reflect an inner transformation: "But the aim of such instruction is love that comes from a pure heart, a good conscience, and sincere faith." (Timothy 1:5)

Just as Jesus challenged the religious and social attitudes of his day, we are encouraged to explore Scripture messages that benefit us spiritually so that we, too, can be in a right relationship with God and live an abundant life filled with hope and promise.

Our spiritual beliefs should provide us with a strong sense of belonging or connection with our Creator – but this sense of oneness does not always come about within rigid or legalistic faith traditions. For many years, alcoholics were considered morally inferior and were often shunned and treated as outcasts. Consequently, they often felt abandoned and unworthy of God's grace. It was not until Bill Wilson, the co-founder of Alcoholics Anonymous, converted the Bible's message into workable guidelines that alcoholics finally believed and accepted the good news of God's unconditional love.

Through the creation of this AA community that emphasized solidarity, compassion, forgiveness and reconciliation, suffering people were healed and renewed through the power of love and acceptance.

Although the primary concepts of the Twelve Step Movement were based on the Judeo-Christian tradition, Bill Wilson preferred to use principles that would appeal to alcoholics whether they had faith or not. The steps are suggested guidelines for a spiritual process that can bring people into a new relationship with God, themselves and their neighbour when practised on a daily basis. The principles help those who struggle with addiction to regain their sense of self-esteem and become viable members of society once again. The Twelve Steps demonstrate in very concrete terms God's message for our modern culture. While they were originally related specifically to alcohol addiction, the principles have now become a popular way of dealing with a wide variety of human experiences, as shown by the many groups that are now using the AA recovery program.

Through the love and acceptance that this program generates, we come to realize that we are not failures – nor are we condemned in the eyes of God. Our addictions are evidence of our spiritual thirst and our need to live in harmony with God's will. This means we must let go of old attitudes and behaviours that have undermined our spiritual well-being. We must be reborn in body, mind and spirit.

In his book *The Sermon on the Mount: The Key to Success in Life*, the scientist, philosopher and spiritual teacher Emmet Fox tells us that the teachings of Jesus in the Sermon on the Mount and the Lord's Prayer give us a concise remedy for the development of the soul. The sermon, which begins with the Beatitudes, summarizes the central theme of Jesus' teachings: the radical transformation of our souls. In order to be in a right relationship with God, we need to acknowledge our spiritual, physical and emotional poverty. Despite our faults and failings, God always hears our pleas and reaches out to us in mercy and love.

The Beatitudes also ask us to reflect on the cost of following Jesus. How much importance have we placed on worshipping the human idols of power, riches, adulation and status? Have we been caught up in an endless striving for perishable and superficial things that eventually leave us empty, weary and dissatisfied? Do we have an insatiable appetite for our drugs of choice, which enslave but do not quench spiritual hunger or thirst? Jesus asks us to reflect on what prevents us from keeping our priorities straight and relying on God as the true source of abundance and comfort.

Jesus wants to set us free and open us up to his love. The freedom he offers doesn't come through power and control but, rather, through the surrender of self-will. This is not an easy message to accept, because we are led to believe that our value comes from our self-sufficiency, reasoning and accomplishments. It is not easy to let go of pride and self-glory in order to humble ourselves and rebuild our lives through faith and dependency on God.

In his interesting and thought-provoking book, Fox tells us that it is hard to be a disciple because, in order to alter our lives and gain health and serenity, we must carry out the spiritual principles of Jesus honestly each day in every area of our lives.

Chapter Five of the Big Book supports Fox's observations and convictions: "Rarely have we seen a person fail who has thoroughly followed our path. Those who do not recover are people who cannot or will not completely give themselves to this simple program, usually men and women who are constitutionally incapable of being honest with themselves."[1]

Let's look at the spiritual principles of the Bible and AA to see how the concepts of surrender, conversion, redemption and reconciliation can promote healing and reinforce honesty, forgiveness, trust and responsibility. Self-will can be a deeply spiritual problem. Until we allow our will to become one with the will of God, we will remain unfulfilled and alienated – not only from God, but from ourselves and from others. Let's examine these spiritual principles and see how they can help us in "the development of the soul" as we begin our process of transformation and rebirth.

You know the insults I receive,
    and my shame and dishonour;
    my foes are all known to you.
Insults have broken my heart,
    so that I am in despair.
I looked for pity, but there was none;
    and for comforters, but I found none.

Psalm 69:19-20

Step One

*We admitted we were powerless over alcohol –
that our lives had become unmanageable.*

Step One can be applied to all addictions – alcohol, drugs, gambling, sex, eating disorders, work or relationships. Probably everyone has experienced powerlessness and unmanageability in one or more of these areas, at one time or another. However, it's not always easy to admit that we have lived in chaos and turmoil, which has had adverse effects on us and on our family, friends and co-workers. When we finally become aware and are able to acknowledge our dysfunctional behaviour, we can concentrate on changing that behaviour and regaining stability in our lives.

A vital part of our recovery as women, however, is not only acknowledging our powerlessness and the unmanageability of our lives, but reclaiming the power to take care of ourselves. The Bible tells us that our body is a temple of the Holy Spirit (1 Corinthians 6:19-20), and that we are obligated to take care of it. When we

23

respect and cherish our bodies, we engage in a healthy and balanced lifestyle. We partake of wholesome food, rest, physical activity, relaxation and spiritual practices. Engaging in self-care also means rejecting needless suffering, self-abasement and compulsive caretaking.

Learning to Love Ourselves

Jesus' primary message was one of love: love of God, love of neighbour and love of self. When we spend an entire lifetime in the service of others, neglecting our own needs and aspirations, we can eventually feel unappreciated, frustrated and angry. This perverts the Christian message.

The more I speak to women about their experiences, the more I realize how much we have in common. Throughout my childhood, I was warned not to become "swell-headed" over my accomplishments or selfish and self-seeking in my behaviour. Like many women, I internalized the message all too well; even now I continue to downplay my own needs and talents. I know I am not alone in thinking that we all would have benefited from lessons in self-love, assertiveness and boundary issues.

When I speak about boundaries, I am referring to the limits we need to set in order to establish realistic, healthy responses to the needs of others. We need to be reasonable about what we will and will not do for others. It is so easy for us to give our time and energy without considering our own needs. Before long, our well-meaning generosity has become compulsive caretaking, and we are left depleted and exhausted. We have a right to say no to the demands of others, but some of us only learn to do so when unreasonable demands undermine our health.

Many women can identify with this plight. We have probably indulged in too much self-sacrifice and now need more self-care. We have to value ourselves for who we are, not just for what we do for others. If we wish to help others, we have to love and tend to ourselves too, because true self-love goes hand in hand with loving others. Being available to others does not mean giving in to all their expectations, because that can invite exploitation and manipulation, which is not in the best interests of either party.

When we study the life of Jesus Christ, we see that while he did much for others, he also took time for solitude and renewal. "But now more than ever the word of Jesus spread abroad; many crowds would gather to hear him and to be cured of their diseases. But he would withdraw to deserted places and pray." (Luke 5:15-16)

Misogyny may not be as overt today as it was in the biblical account of Lot's willingness to sacrifice his virgin daughters; nevertheless, it prevails. Some of the qualities extolled by church and society – such as submissiveness, obedience and gentleness – encourage us to be passive, and can be detrimental to our health and self-esteem. In an effort to please, we often do whatever is asked of us. We stifle our own valid opinions and abdicate power to think, feel and act. We bear our pain in silence, never communicating our feelings in an honest, forthright manner. The suffering that women experience as victims of violence, poverty and abuse is rooted in the subordinate status dictated by a system that once perceived women as chattels, subject to subordination and domination. Some traditions continue to reinforce the oppression of women by assigning a positive, redemptive quality to suffering and victimization.

Taking Charge

When women today are conditioned to sacrifice themselves for the well-being of others, they often stay in destructive, unhealthy relationships and situations. We must reject this concept and stop accepting needless suffering as God's will. Working towards reconciliation is worthwhile in relationships that have some positive qualities. However, for women who live in terror, reconciliation is not possible. These women may refuse to end dangerous partnerships because of conventional beliefs, financial security, fear or resignation. Needless suffering produces feelings of hopelessness, worthlessness, self-doubt and self-hate, which are the opposite of trust, faith, and the creative and redemptive suffering of Christ, which promises resurrection and new life. While it is true that Jesus suffers with the victims of physical, sexual, psychological and economic abuse, he does not cause or approve of that suffering.

Consider the story of Anne, a woman who stayed in an abusive marriage for ten years. Her alcoholic husband was jealous, verbally demeaning and domineering. Since Anne had been brought up in an alcoholic home, where she saw her father verbally and physically abuse her mother, she was familiar with this scenario and accepted it as normal. She even came to believe she deserved this type of treatment because she was not living up to her husband's expectations. Anne was a talented, intelligent woman who gave up her career in order to appease her husband. She had worked primarily with men and he was afraid she would be unfaithful to him. When she wanted to return to university, he vetoed that on similar grounds. Because of his obsessive jealousy, Anne put aside her projects and dreams so that her husband would not feel threatened by her creative or vocational interests. As Anne began to withdraw from life, her self-esteem eroded and she became lonely, depressed and suicidal. Fortunately, there came a point where she could not tolerate his dominance any longer; she summoned the courage to tell him that she was leaving the marriage. He threatened to kill her and their children if she did, but she left anyway. She went to a home for battered women, and eventually divorced him and reclaimed her life.

Empowerment can be a difficult issue for women because whenever we take responsibility for our welfare, by confronting or resisting oppressive situations, there will be an adverse reaction to our new assertiveness. Others may not approve of the health-promoting choices that we make to advance and protect our recovery. They may judge us as being selfish and self-centred. When we refuse to be mistreated and start to expect equality in our relationships, when we attend a Twelve Step meeting, a women's support group or a therapy session, we are making a commitment to self-love. We are learning to acknowledge our self-worth and reclaim our power. The first year in recovery may be punctuated by crises as the people involved relate to each other in new ways. If family members, friends or colleagues are not participating in Twelve Step support groups, they may feel threatened or confused by the altered dynamics in relationships – even (or especially) if the quality of our lives shows a marked improvement. Without a doubt, when we set boundaries that defy the status quo, we will experience resistance and there will be a cost.

In her book *Beyond Anger*, Carolyn Osiek talks about the high price women pay when they discover a new perspective, where what was once acceptable is acceptable no longer. She calls this an intellectual conversion, a conscious assumption of our own power. It is a turning away from the "sin of passivity" and from acquiescence in our own oppression. She states that although there is suffering in authentic human growth and transformation, it is not passive but redemptive.[2] The story of Queen Vashti (Esther 1:10-22) vividly illustrates this point.

Queen Vashti would not degrade herself by agreeing to her husband's demand that she flaunt her beauty before his drunken courtiers. Vashti's decision not only exposed the moral chaos in the royal court but also challenged the king's authority. Because the officials feared that other women would soon follow her example, she was considered a threat to society. In her courageous effort to confront a corrupt system and defend her dignity, Vashti became a victim of injustice. She was stripped of her regal position and banished from the court.

In a society that venerated men, Queen Vashti was considered her husband's property; he could treat her as he wished. She had no rights and could not defend or protect herself against his demands. Despite Vashti's fall, her story is still one of empowerment. I see her as a heroine, a woman who would not passively defer to the king or trade her self-worth in order to maintain her royal status and security. In a society where a husband could divorce his wife for no apparent reason, she was not afraid to claim her voice and honour her body. A woman who retained her integrity and claimed her power despite the consequences, she makes a good role model for women today.

Queen Vashti reminds me of Joan, a woman I met some years ago. She lived in a country-club setting, travelled abroad, wore designer clothes and hobnobbed with the rich and famous. Despite the fact that she had all the trappings that money can buy, she was a battered wife whose sense of self-worth was constantly eroded by the beatings she endured. To combat depression, Joan filled her days with compulsive shopping, redecorating, social activities and alcohol. When she realized her drinking was becoming a problem, she questioned why she was staying in the marriage and became more honest with herself. She was not staying because she loved her husband but because she valued the financial security and was afraid to be on her own.

When Joan finally ended the marriage, she was surprised at the number of people who avoided her. Even though she had left with good reason, she felt stigmatized. Some of her friends thought she had lost her senses, that there must be something wrong with her to leave a handsome husband, wealth and prestige. No one imagined that she might have had legitimate, healthy reasons for what she did. Nevertheless, because of her courage, she was able to reclaim her self-worth and dignity.

As women, we need to understand that although outside forces will try to sabotage new recovery behaviours, we, too, sometimes undermine our own potential for growth. Recovery requires effort and dedication. We may become frustrated with the amount of time it takes to pursue this path. When we begin the process, deeply ingrained messages from the past will surface to persuade us that we are being selfish and don't have the right to play an active role in the way our lives unfold. We have to release these negative thoughts, or they will keep us locked into shame, guilt, fear, self-doubt and complacency.

After years of addiction and destructive choices, we can now comprehend our sacredness and treat ourselves with respect as we take responsibility for our welfare in a healthy manner.

After admitting and accepting that our lives have been out of control, we are now ready to reflect on Step Two and the restoration of sanity.

You will not fear the terror of the night,
    or the arrow that flies by day,
or the pestilence that stalks in darkness,
    or the destruction that wastes at noonday....

Because you have made the LORD your refuge,
    the Most High your dwelling place,
no evil shall befall you,
    no scourge come near your tent.

Psalm 91:5-10

Step Two

*Came to believe that a Power greater than
ourselves could restore us to sanity.*

When we read Step Two and the words "restore us
to sanity," our initial reaction may be indigna-
tion. We may become upset that anyone would imply
that we are not sane, but if we know that the definition
of sanity is "soundness of mind or judgment" then we
may recognize that we do not always handle our problems
rationally. When we are in the throes of addiction, we
do not see how our coping mechanisms blind us from
the truth and allow us to justify our actions. Irrational
thinking and dysfunctional behaviour appear in many
guises but, in all instances, when we cling tenaciously to
misguided ideas, beliefs and conduct, we hinder our spiritual growth. A condensed version of Irma's story will
show what I mean.

    Irma was a self-assured, well-educated, successful
businesswoman. She was active in the community; when
a project needed to be done promptly and efficiently,

people called Irma. Despite this glowing public image, her personal life left much to be desired. She was a closet alcoholic. She was bored and disenchanted with her marriage, and she could not sustain friendships. This was primarily due to her self-absorption, which deeply impaired her ability to empathize with the problems and needs of others.

Irma saw herself as a free spirit and liberal thinker. In fact, she was a very critical and judgmental person who would readily point out the faults of others in harsh, abusive terms. Paradoxically, she was oblivious to her own character defects and their effect on others. A biblical passage from the New Testament described her well: "Why do you see the speck in your neighbour's eye, but do not notice the log in your own eye?" (Luke 6:41) One particular woman was the brunt of many cruel remarks because of a trivial breach of etiquette that had offended Irma's sensibilities. The irony was that Irma was engaged in an affair with this woman's husband. Irma didn't seem to be troubled by the morality of this liaison at all. On the contrary, she condoned and rationalized her behaviour; it was obvious that her liberal outlook on life came to the fore when it suited her own needs and purposes. Irma refused to evaluate her life in order to change.

When we become humble enough to examine our actions, we can see that irrational thinking and rigid habits are dominant character traits. We may be appalled to see that we have engaged in dysfunctional behaviour time and time again, unable to comprehend why we experience the same futile, damaging results repeatedly. Some of us become exhausted from self-neglect and anxiety, accompanied by a sense of isolation due to misunderstandings with family and friends.

Melody Beattie, an addictions counsellor, has compiled an extensive list of these rigid character traits in her book *Codependent No More*. These include the following: caretaking, low self-worth, repression, obsession, controlling, denial, dependency, poor communication, weak boundaries, lack of trust, anger and sex problems. She calls the personality type engaged in these dysfunctional behaviours "codependent," which she describes as one who allows another person's actions to affect him or her, and in so doing becomes obsessed with controlling that person's behaviour.

Codependent No More was on the *New York Times* bestseller list for three years, and with good reason. It resonates with all women who have neglected their physical, emotional and spiritual needs in order to please someone else. It speaks to women who have become obsessed with their relationships and have lost themselves in the process, exhausted women who continue to give when they are the ones in need of nurturing. These are women who do not know how to say "Enough is enough; I'm tired." Instead, they judge themselves harshly if they cannot complete everything on their "must do" list.

Relationships are important to women; we desire the approval of others. Nevertheless, we must let go of the self-defeating conviction that our worth is defined by endless caretaking, which can encourage deprivation as a way of life. We have to acknowledge that when we are true to ourselves and take responsibility for our choices, those choices will not please everyone. We must remember that we are good people, and that our healthy behaviours are not self-indulgence but the path to the higher good of all involved.

We must also stop believing that our worth and identity are defined by the people or things we are involved with. We cannot attain these from outside ourselves. When our self-worth and identity rest on being in a relationship, we reinforce our dependency and vulnerability, and relinquish power because we fear loss. We turn ourselves inside out in order to hold onto a relationship, and in our needy desperation our sense of self disappears as we cater to another's needs.

We, as women, have to accept ourselves and find happiness within. We must nourish our own interests rather than deferring to others, and stop the endless wait for the right person to come along and validate our existence. We are complete just as we are, whether or not we have a partner.

For years many of us have lived within the suffocating, restrictive cocoon of addiction. Our illusions and denial have caused us to acquiesce and participate in unhealthy, reckless behaviour. When addictive impulses control the mind, memory can be quite selective. We remember the highs and the good times, but forget the insidious entrapment and disintegration of mind, body and spirit. I've heard women say that after undergoing an assessment of their chemical use, they can't believe they are alive today. Some have overdosed, driven while intoxicated or gone into dangerous neighbourhoods to obtain drugs. Others have resorted to shoplifting and stealing from family members and friends in order to get money to support their habit. One woman said she really knew her life had become insane when she was arrested for shoplifting and possession of drugs.

Step Two offers a ray of hope, a promise of new life. It is a tremendous relief when we come to believe that a "Power greater than ourselves" specifically intends to restore us to sanity and free us from the crushing burden of our tormented and limited existence. It is a redemptive experience when we act upon Jesus' invitation to "Come and see," and enter into a deeper relationship with him (John 1:39). When we realize it is time to change, to reclaim our lives, we begin the process of healing and transformation. It seems like scales have been removed from our eyes, or we have risen from a deep sleep. Like the blind man in the Gospel of John, we eventually proclaim, "One thing I do know, that though I was blind, now I see." (John 9:25)

This dependence on a Higher Power, however, requires the total surrender of our self-will to the will of God. In the Big Book, the phrase "self-will run riot" describes our false pride and inability to see the powerlessness of our lives. Our insanity rests in the fact that our addiction became our higher power even though it had created havoc with our lives.

Initially, this "letting go and letting God" may seem frightening – until we consider the alternative. When we revisit our past and recall fear, frustration, shame, chaos and desperation, I believe we'll be unanimous in deciding to give Step Three a try. We have nothing to lose and much to gain – peace and serenity. When we accept the blessings of this supportive and renewing process, we begin the journey home to our true creative selves.

The LORD will guide you continually,
        and satisfy your needs in parched places,
        and make your bones strong;
and you shall be like a watered garden,
        like a spring of water,
        whose waters never fail.

Isaiah 58:11

Step Three

Made a decision to turn our will and our lives over to the care of God as we understood Him.

Steps Two and Three may be perceived as stumbling blocks if they are associated with abusive or negative religious beliefs or experiences. As children, we may have been given the image of a distant, punitive God whose primary purpose was to dispense punishment to sinful people. "God is going to punish you for being bad," we may have been told. This fed into our sense of shame, and so we felt unworthy of God's love and forgiveness. Because of this misconception, many of us have removed and isolated ourselves from our one true source of strength and comfort.

However, we now have the opportunity to re-evaluate our beliefs and, if necessary, change our image or concept of our Higher Power. Step Three tells us that we are turning our will and our lives over to the God of our understanding. Since our spiritual journey is a quest for truth, this step allows us the flexibility to explore our concept of the Divine Spirit from as many creative perspectives as we choose. This step restores our faith in a God who cares and blesses us. It gives us permission to reject the punitive, shaming, relentless taskmaster of our youth. We now choose to surrender our will and our lives to a benevolent Spirit who loves and nurtures us. "Cast all your anxiety on him, because he cares for you." (1 Peter 5:7)

In the Gospel of Luke, Jesus presents us with three parables – The Lost Sheep, The Lost Coin, and The Prodigal Son (Luke 15:1-32) – all of which illustrate a concerned God searching for what is lost and celebrating when it is found. In the story of the Prodigal Son, the wayward son who has squandered his fortune on a life of debauchery is welcomed back into his father's household with love, forgiveness and rejoicing. This parable can be viewed not only as the story of a son who has strayed but also as the story of a way of life that was embraced and later proved to be barren, debilitating and meaningless. The simple sensitivity of these parables shows us the redeeming quality of God's unconditional love. Numerous passages contained in the Gospel of John also help us understand the importance of unconditional love in our recovery process. "As the Father has loved me, so I have loved you; abide in my love…. This is my commandment, that you love one another as I have loved you." (John 15:9-12) When we can accept that God loves and accepts us unconditionally, we gradually begin to love ourselves. Our world becomes friendlier, more peaceful and serene.

Knowing that, as a prodigal daughter, I was still loved and validated has made a tremendous difference in my life. With the confidence of St. Paul, I now pray that by being "rooted and grounded in love," I will continue to know that Christ dwells in my heart and to experience the love that surpasses knowledge (Ephesians 3:17-19). Step Three gave me permission to re-examine my beliefs, discard my false image of God and dethrone a vindictive idol who held me in the bondage of fear. I replaced this image with that of a merciful God.

Raised in Fear

Fear began in my childhood. I was born into an Italian Roman Catholic family where submissive, passive behaviour was considered a virtue. As a child, my concept of God was a bearded old man in the sky who kept a daily ledger of my venial and mortal sins. At that time, when one committed a mortal sin one's salvation was considered to be in grave danger. For instance, if I chose to stay in bed on a Sunday morning rather than attend Mass, and if perchance I died before confessing this sin and receiving absolution, I believed I would go straight to hell.

Throughout my early years, I tried hard to please this distant God. I erected a little altar in my bedroom, where a crucifix and a statue of the Blessed Virgin Mary stood beside my favourite saint, Anthony of Padua, the patron saint of lost things. I knelt before this altar morning and evening, praying that I would become good enough to be a nun one day. All my devotions, novenas and penances never seemed enough, however. I never felt that I could attain the perfection required to receive God's mercy. I could not describe these feelings of being less than, or fundamentally flawed. (Today, these would be called shame-based.) I didn't feel secure in my world, and because I could not articulate my feelings of inadequacy, there was no one to comfort me or share my pain.

I had always believed that obeying God's word meant following rigid rules, working and being super-efficient in order to get merit points in God's record book. I have now come to realize how distorted my thinking was and how harshly I judged myself. Slowly, I have let go of the unrealistic standards that set me up for failure. "Progress, not perfection" has become my motto; I have come to see myself as lovable and acceptable despite my imperfections and limitations. Again, I am grateful for the words of Paul that have enlightened me: "For by grace you have been saved through faith, and this is not your own doing; it is the gift of God – not the result of works, so that no one may boast." (Ephesians 2:8-9)

When I was a child, my biblical knowledge was limited to the Scripture readings I heard at Mass. When I finally began to read the Bible for myself, I was amazed at how often Jesus tried to change the Pharisees' image of God from one of vengeance to one of compassion. This is clearly shown in the gospel narratives concerning the Mosaic Law (Exodus 35:2) that forbade any type of activity or work on the Sabbath. A violation of this law was punishable by death.

One Sabbath, Jesus' hungry disciples were caught picking corn in a field and were criticized by the Pharisees. Jesus defended his disciples, and rebuked the Pharisees for their zealous preoccupation with rules. In doing so, Jesus proclaimed the dignity of humankind. The needs of the people were to take precedence over the Law; for this reason, he continued to perform miracles and acts of charity on the Sabbath. The Pharisees, immersed in their scrupulous religiosity and adherence to the letter of the Law, viewed the needs of the people as secondary. They interpreted the compassionate words and actions of Jesus as sacrilegious, a threat to the status quo. The Pharisees' tragedy was that their obsessive attachment to self-serving religious routines prevented them from accepting God's greatest gift to the world – the gift of grace. That is how they stifled spiritual freedom and growth.

In many respects, I once had much in common with the Pharisees. I, too, had been caught up in a regimen that focused on fear, sin and punishment. I had overlooked the fact that "God is love" and "There is no fear in love, but perfect love casts out fear; for fear has to do with punishment and whoever fears has not reached perfection in love." (1 John 4:16-18) This love manifested itself on the cross, when Jesus forgave his unrepentant executioners as he was dying: "Father, forgive them; for they do not know what they are doing." (Luke 23:34)

I needed to hear these messages of love and forgiveness, and I needed to know that I did not have to be perfect in order to be loved and forgiven. Jesus came to heal, not punish, and his mercy is freely given. It was a revelation when I saw how my image of God and self were so closely related. When I was able to change my image of God to one of compassion, I became less critical of and kinder to myself. I am now able to receive the divine gift of grace, which is very important for my spiritual journey.

Although God is the sustaining power of love in our universe, God is also spirit – and thus the ultimate mystery, one that is beyond our limited comprehension. "God is spirit, and those who worship him must worship in spirit and truth." (John 4:24) "No one has ever seen God; if we love one another, God lives in us, and his love is perfected in us." (1 John 4:12)

A New Perspective

Seeking the God of our understanding can be both a sacred and a liberating experience as we discover new ways to discern spiritual truths and wisdom. If we read the Bible from a feminine perspective, we can envision the Spirit of God to be expansive enough to include both feminine and masculine imagery. "So God created humankind in his image, in the image of God he created them; male and female he created them." (Genesis 1:27)

Many women in recovery have been sexually abused by men they have trusted – such as their fathers, grandfathers, uncles, brothers, cousins or family friends, as well as men in professions of trust – so they have a hard time with the masculine image of God. When Marnie was sexually abused by her father, a prominent businessman and church elder in their small community, her concept of a loving and caring God was completely shattered. "Where was God when I was being abused year after year? Why didn't God come to my rescue when I prayed for protection? I have given up on God, since I cannot bear the thought of a male God," she told me bitterly.

One of the most difficult aspects of my Twelve Step ministry was listening to the stories of women who have endured incest and sexual abuse; their ordeals have carved a huge spiritual void within them. It has left them with a profound sense of shame, and the belief that their bodies and souls have been desecrated, that they are now damaged goods.

The Old Testament story of Tamar, King David's daughter, resonates with these women. Tamar is betrayed and raped by her brother, Amnon, and then rejected. Her brother, Absalom, learns of the atrocity but tells her to remain silent about it. "Be quiet for now, my sister; he is your brother; do not take this to heart." (2 Samuel 13:14-20) Thus the rape is discounted, and the desolate Tamar carries her shame in her wounded heart and violated body.

Tamar's story is quite common among women who come to treatment centres to deal with their addictions. They have kept their secrets well, or if they did disclose them to family members, they often found themselves ostracized and seen as liars or troublemakers. This victimized them once again. It is not surprising, then, that they turn to alcohol, drugs or food to relieve their deep pain and despair.

A number of abused women have found the images of God as a mother of wisdom and understanding helpful in their healing process. "Happy are those who find wisdom, and those who get understanding…. Her ways are ways of pleasantness, and all her paths are peace. She is a tree of life to those who lay hold of her…. If you sit down, you will not be afraid; when you lie down, your sleep will be sweet." (Proverbs 3:13-24)

The beautiful feminine imagery in the Book of Isaiah is very nurturing. "Can a woman forget her nursing child, or show no compassion for the child of her womb? Even these may forget, yet I will not forget you. See, I have inscribed you on the palms of my hands." (Isaiah 49:15-16) In Part Two of this book, I have provided more feminine images of God as a woman, mother and Divine Wisdom, the feminine presence who was with God from the beginning of time (Proverbs 8:22-31).

For some abused women, the masculinity of God has not been a problem. They like the compassionate way Jesus treated women. They felt that because Jesus was betrayed by someone he trusted and because he, too, suffered the agonies of violation, he could identify and be with them in their suffering. They see Jesus as a source of healing and renewal.

Since the Divine Spirit can never be fully known, I have told these women that how they define God is not as important as being aware of a loving presence in their lives, and developing a trusting relationship with the God of their understanding. Since the Divine Spirit can never be fully known, I have suggested that they release harmful images of God and open their hearts to this Divine Love, comfort and support. In the Old Testament, God's name is a verb: "I AM WHO I AM." (Exodus 3:14) The Book of Revelation declares: "I am the Alpha and the Omega," says the Lord God, "who is and who was and who is to come, the Almighty." (Revelation 1:8) These models describe a God of action who is in our midst and involved in our lives. The words of St. Paul describe it eloquently: "In him we live and move and have our being.... For we too are his offspring." (Acts

17:28) No matter what terminology we choose to describe the Divine Spirit, it is always about a relationship of love. This makes a profound difference in our self-esteem when we perceive ourselves as beloved daughters of God.

Children of God

I believe that being known as God's "offspring" is essential to our spiritual welfare. Women who have been abused and betrayed by family members have had to grieve the loss of their expectations of what an ideal family should be, as well as their loss of innocence and the protection that should have been their birthright. Since their earthly families did not support them, it is good for them to know that God is a faithful parent who can be trusted. Jesus defined true kinship not in biological terms, but this way: "Whoever does the will of God is my brother and sister and mother." (Mark 3:35) The healing process begins when we connect with our spiritual family, the people we can relate to – whether that be through Christian fellowship, a recovery group or both.

The decision to turn our will and our lives over to God calls for us to let go of our illusions of control and detach from all that separates us from God's will, as our addictions have done. Our spiritual quest for God has been replaced by our obsessive need for our drug of choice. We have searched for God in all the wrong places. Only God can quench our spiritual thirst. "Let anyone who is thirsty come to me, and let the one who believes in me drink. As the Scripture has said, 'Out of the believer's heart shall flow rivers of living water.'" (John 7:37-38)

The ministry of Jesus Christ was a manifestation of God's love on earth. It is not surprising, then, that Steps One, Two and Three discuss letting go of our destructive self-will, which has robbed us of God's love and creative energy. We have to relinquish former lives of enslavement and alienation in order to be reborn and empowered by God's liberating grace and renewing Spirit. Paul wrote: "Do not be conformed to this world, but be transformed by the renewing of your minds, so that you may discern what is the will of God – what is good and acceptable and perfect." (Romans 12:2) The Serenity Prayer tells us to accept the things we cannot change, and allow ourselves to become receptive to God's wisdom so that we, with courage, may change the things we can. Serenity will never be ours as long as we are controlled by self-will.

The Third Step Prayer also speaks of surrender and serenity:

> God, I offer myself to Thee – to build with me and to do with me as Thou wilt. Relieve me of the bondage of self, that I may better do Thy will. Take away my difficulties, that victory over them may bear witness to those I would help of Thy Power, Thy Love, and Thy Way of Life. May I do Thy will always![3]

Having turned ourselves over to God's care, we are now ready to live in the present moment. When we live one day at a time, we can concentrate on making each day better. We can let go of remorse and fear, and embrace each moment with faith and hope. Various passages in the Bible support the adage of living one day at a time. The Lord's Prayer is the most universal, but one discourse in Matthew also gives Jesus' viewpoint on the futility of wasting precious energy in needless worry about the future.

> "Therefore I tell you, do not worry about your life, what you will eat or what you will drink, or about your body, what you will wear.... your heavenly Father knows that you need all these things. But strive first for the kingdom of God and his righteousness, and all these things will be given to you as well. So do not worry about tomorrow, for tomorrow will bring worries of its own. Today's trouble is enough for today." (Matthew 6:25-34)

Jesus is directing us to develop a spirit of absolute trust in God. This does not imply immature, irresponsible or demanding behaviour on our part, nor does it imply that our relationship is to be one of passive dependence. He is not suggesting that we use God as a magical daily Santa Claus. Although we are asked to call on God for clarity and direction in evaluating our plans and decisions, we are required to do the spadework and leave the outcome to God. For instance, if we need guidance concerning our education or career, we pray for discernment in making our choices. Then we obtain the appropriate education, prepare resumes, attend job interviews and surrender the outcome to Divine Wisdom. This is what Jesus asks of us when we align our lives and our will to the will of

God in an intimate and co-operative partnership that sustains us on a daily basis.

Now that we have surrendered and turned our lives and our will over to God, we can begin our spiritual journey into self-discovery and disclosure. In Steps Four and Five, we look at both the negative aspects of our personalities as well as positive character traits, such as our goodness, gifts and blessings.

O Lord, you have searched me and known me.
You know when I sit down and when I rise up;
    you discern my thoughts from far away.
You search out my path and my lying down,
    and are acquainted with all my ways.
Even before a word is on my tongue,
    O Lord, you know it completely.

Psalm 139:1-4

Step Four

Made a searching and fearless moral inventory of ourselves.

Step Five

Admitted to God, to ourselves and to another human being the exact nature of our wrongs.

Each one of the Twelve Steps sets the foundation for the next, so there is continuity and a logical progression. I have chosen to combine, in pairs, the next six steps because they are so interrelated. In Step Four, we are encouraged to write down our stories in an honest and forthright manner because that allows us to see ourselves exactly as we are, and prevents us from fudging the truth. Since the inventories are personal, we are to focus on *our* involvement in the painful events of our lives, even though we may not be totally at fault. Our written evaluations are not quite enough, however. Step Five asks us to share our stories with another person. Both steps are meant to liberate us from guilt and shame as we come to terms with our past and assess whether we are now becoming the Spirit-filled people God wants us to be.

Steps Four and Five require that we submit to authentic soul-searching. Without a doubt, this procedure will be extremely painful and will demand courage and perseverance as we fearlessly take our inventories. In the process of unmasking our deepest secrets and character defects, we may be overcome with remorse and tempted to dwell on negative aspects of our lives while glossing over or negating our positive attributes. While an honest appraisal is very important to the recovery process, we must not obsess over faults and failures, or we might become discouraged and despondent. It is far better to look upon these steps as an exercise in accountability and a measure of our spiritual development as we grow in self-awareness and honesty.

Telling All

As a chaplain, I have listened to many Fifth Steps. A few women have glossed over their negative characteristics and behaviours. They embellished or withheld the truth, and because their defence mechanisms were intact, they remained out of touch with reality. Refusal to undertake a fearless moral inventory prevented them from seeing how pride, arrogance, dishonesty, selfishness and lack of compassion were hindering their spiritual growth. Irma, the woman I described in Step Two, would fit into this category. She would also fit the description in Chapter Five of the Big Book of one who may not recover: "men and women who are constitutionally incapable of becoming honest with themselves."

Many women, however, tend to be scrupulous and shame-based when they admit their failings. They are overly conscious of their faults and imperfections and thus need others to point out their positive qualities. We must differentiate between shame and guilt here. Shame has to do with our identity; it is an inner sense of being inadequate and unworthy. It is internalized and continually tells us that we are not good enough. Thus the issue becomes not what we have done but what we *are* as persons. We do not like, accept or respect ourselves. Shame is a form of false pride, because when we reject our goodness we are saying, in essence, that we are too horrible and sinful to receive God's grace and forgiveness.

Guilt, on the other hand, is the legitimate pain or regret we feel when our behaviour has violated our moral code. The appropriate response is some form of acknowledgment and reparation. Although we are sorry for our actions, our core sense of self remains intact; we do not reject ourselves. Both guilt and shame can keep us from becoming well unless we accept our humanity and develop an attitude of unconditional love, acceptance and forgiveness as we learn self-appreciation in an imperfect world.

In disclosing our stories, we will likely feel apprehensive. The exposure, combined with personal guilt, shame and low self-esteem, may leave us feeling vulnerable to ridicule, rejection or punishment. We must keep in mind, however, that a Fifth Step listener will probably be a clergy person, a respected member of the AA community, or someone who has a working knowledge of the Twelve Step program – a trustworthy confidant who will be non-judgmental and sensitive to our discomfort.

When we share our inventories with one another, we grow in self-knowledge because our listener will help us to clarify issues and see them from a new perspective. When self-examination and disclosure are done with utmost honesty and integrity, they can lead to spiritual healing. This is our road to freedom, because in releasing our toxic secrets, we release feelings of alienation and despair. We can then seek reconciliation with God, our neighbour and ourselves.

Vanquishing Anger and Guilt

When we participate in Steps Four and Five, we are often surprised to see how anger and resentment have played havoc with our spiritual progress. It is important, therefore, to spend some time concentrating on these emotions. The Big Book emphasizes the importance of dealing with resentment.

> Resentment is the "number one" offender. It destroys more alcoholics than anything else. From it stem all forms of spiritual disease, for we have been not only mentally and physically ill, we have been spiritually sick.[4]

The remedy for this malady is also contained in the Big Book:

If you have a resentment you want to be free of, if you will pray for the person or the thing that you resent, you will be free. If you will ask in prayer for everything you want for yourself to be given to them, you will be free. Ask for their health, their prosperity, their happiness, and you will be free. Even when you don't really want it for them, and your prayers are only words and you don't mean it, go ahead and do it anyway. Do it every day for two weeks and you will find you have come to mean it and to want it for them, and you will realize that where you used to feel bitterness and resentment and hatred, you now feel compassionate understanding and love.[5]

The Bible, too, has abundant advice to give regarding anger and the optimum goals of repentance, forgiveness and reconciliation. "Refrain from anger, and forsake wrath. Do not fret – it leads only to evil." (Psalm 37:8) In the Lord's Prayer, we hear Jesus saying: "And forgive us our debts, as we also have forgiven our debtors.... For if you forgive others their trespasses, your heavenly Father will also forgive you; but if you do not forgive others, neither will your Father forgive your trespasses." (Matthew 6:12-15) Jesus makes no concessions, nor does he offer any alternatives. The simple fact is that if we do not forgive, we will not be forgiven.

People who have been sexually, physically, emotionally, psychologically or spiritually abused will often say that they will never forgive their perpetrators. In these instances, I suggest that they ask God to be their intermediary and do the forgiving for them until they are able to obtain the spiritual strength to accomplish this independently.

Forgiveness can also be especially difficult in cases of divorce. Divorce is traumatic at any time, but for women who have been married for thirty or forty years and have made marriage their lifelong vocation, it can be devastating. Divorce in this circumstance is a shameful, humiliating experience and a blow to self-esteem.

Thelma was sixty years old and had been married for forty years when her husband asked for a divorce. These are the words she used to describe her pain:

> I was raised in an era when a woman of marriageable age was taught that a good wife had to subordinate her needs to those of her husband and family, so I became that good wife. I was at my husband's beck and call. Whatever he wanted, I did. Then, after living through economic hardships, the difficult teen years, and numerous hospitalizations, I thought we could start to enjoy life and do the things we had had to put on hold. Instead, he drops his bombshell and tells me he is leaving me for another woman. Our marriage meant everything to me. I feel like such a failure! How do I start over again at this late stage of my life?

I have heard many heartbreaking stories like Thelma's. When the person you have loved, trusted and shared half a lifetime with deserts you, the shock and grief can be unbearable. King David expressed it well: "It is not enemies who taunt me – I could bear that; it is not adversaries who deal insolently with me – I could hide from them. But it is you, my equal, my companion, my familiar friend, with whom I kept pleasant company...." (Psalm 55:12-14) The harm inflicted upon us by someone we love is always harder to bear, and divorce brings home the stark reality that marriage vows do not always come with a lifetime guarantee. The one guarantee we do have is of God's fidelity: "And remember, I am with you always, to the end of the age." (Matthew 28:20)

Thelma and others in similar situations must go through the intense pain of rejection and grieve this loss; but, ultimately, these women will have to make peace within themselves. This is not easy, and often our faith is tested to the max as we face the reality that life will never be the same again. This may mean living alone and giving up cherished dreams. Our solitude, however, can become an opportunity for spiritual growth and a time to honour and value our unique gifts as we gradually come to accept and rebuild our lives as single women. I found the following poem very consoling when I was going through a time of grief.

> After a while, you learn the subtle difference between holding a hand and chaining a soul –
>
> And you learn that love doesn't mean leaning and company doesn't mean security –
>
> And you begin to learn that kisses aren't contracts and presents aren't promises –
>
> And you begin to accept your defeats with your head up and your eyes opened, with the grace of an adult, not the grief of a child –

And you learn to build your roads on today because tomorrow's ground is too uncertain for plans –

After a while you learn that even sunshine burns if you get too much –

So you plant your own garden and decorate your own soul instead of waiting for someone to bring you flowers –

And you learn that you really can endure … that you really are strong and you really do have worth.

Anonymous

As difficult as forgiveness may be in these circumstances, when we refuse to forgive we are hurting ourselves. Until we forgive, our lives will be controlled by resentment and we will be consumed by pain. Forgiveness takes away another person's power to control our emotions. It takes a generous spirit to forgive, to admit that what happened to us was heartbreaking, and to realize that we would be foolish to suffer further by clinging to our resentments. I am always amazed at the generosity of spirit Jesus exhibited when he met Judas in the Garden of Gethsemane. He addressed Judas, who had betrayed and forfeited their friendship for thirty pieces of silver, as a friend: "Friend, do what you are here to do." (Matthew 26:50)

Forgiving a person who has hurt or harmed us does not mean that we accept or condone their actions, or that we have to like or befriend them. It does mean, however, that we are obliged to wish them well and not wish them harm. We are obliged to love and forgive them in order to free ourselves from bitterness and resentment, which would ultimately destroy us. When our hearts are broken and we are hurt and angry, we may feel that our spouses or abusers do not deserve forgiveness. In the ongoing process of forgiveness, we will have to bring our pain to God many times in order to heal, and not be consumed by bitterness.

It is also helpful to remember that anger is a normal response to the various forms of violence, injustice, cruelty, exploitation and abuse that occur daily in our society. It is appropriate to be angry and to dissipate our anger constructively. "Be angry but do not sin; do not let the sun go down on your anger." (Ephesians 4:26)

Because most of us dislike conflict, we avoid it at all costs. However, when we do not acknowledge our grievances and deal with them in a constructive manner, we are in danger of letting them fester. We mishandle grievances when we allow them to dominate our lives or pretend that they do not exist. In the former situation, our anger is quite noticeable. In the latter, repressed anger may not be visible, but it will surface indirectly at the wrong time or place, or directed at the wrong person.

We must validate our anger by expressing it in a healthy way so that we do not harm ourselves or others. The body, mind and spirit are synchronized: what affects one affects the other. Unresolved anger is dangerous not only to arteries, bones and internal organs but, as both Scripture and the Big Book tell us, to our spiritual life as well.

We cannot let anger disguise itself as self-blame, guilt or depression. Awareness of anger is the first step; then we have to decide how we want to respond to it. We may want to communicate our grievances directly to the person involved, or we may find that a good listener is all that is needed. Since every situation is different, our responses will vary. Along with the Bible and the Big Book principles, many other books offer suggestions on how to accept and express anger in a helpful, forthright manner. (Some of these are listed in the Bibliography.)

When we are willing to participate in the Fourth and Fifth Steps with honesty and integrity, we transform our lives and begin true kinship with God, another human being and ourselves. In releasing the burdens of resentment, shame and guilt and replacing them with acceptance, forgiveness and self-love, we gain serenity – and a firm foundation for the remaining six steps.

Have mercy on me, O God
according to your steadfast love;
according to your abundant mercy
blot out my transgressions.
Wash me thoroughly from my iniquity,
and cleanse me from my sin.

Psalm 51:1-2

Step Six

Were entirely ready to have God remove all these defects of character.

Step Seven

Humbly asked Him to remove our shortcomings.

Strange as this may seem, we may not want to part with our negative attitudes and habits, our "pet sins." Even though they have continuously played havoc with our lives, they have nevertheless become comfortable, predictable companions. Although we have made an honest evaluation of our mistakes, weaknesses and indiscretions, there is always resistance to hearing that we must allow God to remove these defects and shortcomings in order to participate fully in our recovery.

At first, it can be intimidating trying to detach ourselves from the things that stand between us and God. We may feel exposed and vulnerable without our familiar coping mechanisms, as we finally realize that denial has blocked out the pain and suffering that we have inflicted on ourselves and on others. Ultimately, we come to accept the fact that if we do not have these character defects and shortcomings removed, we will continue to operate in the same destructive mode. "You were taught to put away your former way of life, your old self, corrupt and deluded by its lusts, and to be renewed in the spirit of your minds, and to clothe yourselves with the new self, created according to the likeness of God in true righteousness and holiness…. Put away from you all bitterness and wrath and anger and wrangling and slander, together with all malice, and be kind to one another, tenderhearted, forgiving one another, as God in Christ has forgiven you." (Ephesians 4:22-32)

We must remember, too, that addictions are outer manifestations of inner anguish and emptiness, our alienation and estrangement from God as well as the inability to love ourselves fully. It is when we humbly ask God to enter into our brokenness to remove our shortcomings that the grace of God is able to transform us, despite our human limitations. In the words of the Big Book:

> My Creator, I am now willing that you should have all of me, good and bad. I pray that you now remove from me every single defect of character which stands in the way of my usefulness to you and my fellows. Grant me strength, as I go out from here, to do your bidding. Amen.[6]

The following meditation describes letting go of our old attitudes and behaviours in order to facilitate transformation and rebirth.

Autumn is a good time to meditate on the deep mysteries of death and transformation. In autumn, the world goes underground. Leaves fall off trees. Days get shorter. Plants turn brown. The world gets dark in preparation for the rebirth of light.

How do we become reborn unless we also allow parts of ourselves to die and fall away? Old ideas, old behaviors, limitations we clung to in the past can now be shed. The person we are dies. We become another person, someone who more closely resembles what we want to become.

For this magical transformation, only willingness is needed. Courage will be supplied. We need only be willing to risk being naked for a time, without our props and familiar routines. We need only be willing to risk finding out more about ourselves.

I willingly surrender. I let go of all old behaviors and beliefs that no longer serve me. I am transformed.[7]

From *The Color of Light* by Perry Tilleraas, copyright 1988 by Hazelden Foundation. Reprinted by permission of Hazelden Foundation, Center City, MN.

The above quotations relate to the biblical principle of dying to self in order to be reborn and have life anew. The term "born again" may sound too moralistic for some, but it does refer to the death and resurrection of our interior lives. It is about letting go of everyone and everything that obstructs or inhibits us from receiving divine love and healing, which we need in order to be transformed.

How We Are Born Anew

Let me tell you a transformation story about a woman I will call Dolly. I have chosen Dolly's story because her sophisticated outward appearance was in such marked contrast to her inner despair. By societal standards, Dolly had everything: she was young, beautiful, wealthy and held a prestigious position in the world of fashion. In reality, though, she was on the fast track to destruction. She had a poor self-image and did not honour herself. She would pick up strange men in bars and go to bed with them. This behaviour resulted in six abortions; complications from these procedures left her unable to have children.

When I met Dolly, she was spiritually bankrupt and had contemplated suicide on a number of occasions. She was filled with remorse, and was convinced that God would never forgive her for the terrible mess she had made of her life. This belief was compounded by the fact that as a child she had been subjected to the ranting of an authoritarian religious leader who used guilt, fear and intimidation to keep his members in line.

Dolly was able to discard the coercive religious beliefs that would have locked her into a punishment mentality, and to accept the gentler gifts of healing, rehabilitation and reconciliation. She engaged in a very painful but honest moral inventory, which allowed her to see both her strengths and her weaknesses. She saw how low self-esteem and irresponsible behaviour had prevented her from understanding and embracing her intrinsic worth as a woman created in the image of God.

Eventually, through extensive counselling, Twelve Step work, prayer and Scripture readings, Dolly regained her confidence and was able to accept God's grace and forgiveness. The reading that had the greatest impact on her was the one about the adulteress whom Jesus did not condemn but forgave and told to sin no more (John 8:1-11). This passage spoke to her of a merciful God who loved her as a person, but was opposed to anything that would destroy her soul.

The principles of recovery apply not only to acts that endanger our well-being, but also to negative thoughts that can harm us. Because Dolly was petrified of relapsing, fear and anxiety were obstacles that she had to address. During the recovery process, negative patterns of thinking and relating are replaced by healthier ones, but it takes time for these patterns to become internalized. Not every chemically dependent person will relapse, but each one is at risk. Our best line of defence, therefore, is to be aware of relapse signs before denial sets in, and we tell ourselves that having a drink or two is harmless, or that after many years of sobriety, AA meetings are tiresome or we have outgrown them.

Stress is another factor that frequently contributes to relapse, so we have to develop effective ways to deal with our problems. Along with being aware of our stressors, we need a safe place to express our emotions. Twelve Step and therapy groups are appropriate places to vent our feelings. Role-playing in therapy groups is another way of coping with stress. This method helps us to see our problems more clearly and enables us to find out what works well for us and what does not. Then, when we find ourselves in similar stressful situations, we have a better understanding of the dynamics and relationship skills we can use.

I told Dolly to be careful whenever feelings that spell out H.A.L.T. – Hungry, Angry, Lonely, Tired – threatened her serenity, and to take remedial action immediately. Any one of these conditions and attitudes can trigger relapse.

Hungry: Because the use of alcohol and drugs often replaces our need for food, a structured, well-balanced and nutritious meal plan has to be integrated into any recovery program. Some nutritionists and therapists believe there is a correlation between susceptibility to alcohol, drug and food abuse and abnormal functioning in the serotonin and endorphin levels of addictive individuals. This, in turn, can result in cravings and an inability to handle stress. In order to alleviate the stress and cravings, we may resort to the empty calories of sweets and junk food or skip meals entirely, and soon our hunger for nurturance is replaced with the urge to indulge in our addiction once again.

Angry: The ways we interact with others can indicate relapse. Are we argumentative and irritable? Are our relationships becoming strained because of our unreasonable demands and resentments, or are we becoming depressed? When we are overwhelmed by these feelings, it is tempting to relieve them by resorting to drugs or alcohol. If we are taking life too seriously and are overcome by stress, it is time to lighten up and develop a sense of humour. Laughter is good for the soul.

Lonely: Loneliness is a serious danger signal for addicts, so a healthy support group is an essential part of recovery. When we attend Twelve Step meetings sporadically or stop entirely, or when we discontinue all treatment, we are cutting ourselves off from a viable source of help. When our patterns of isolation and avoidance are evident, and when compulsive behaviour is reactivated, the risk of returning to former friends, social haunts, alcohol and drugs is not far behind.

Tired: Exhaustion can be another warning signal. If we are prone to overwork or become overly involved in activities, we can set ourselves up for exhaustion and susceptibility to viral infections and illnesses. Proper rest and relaxation are also important because when we are tired or feeling unwell, we are more likely to make mistakes in judgment; our thinking can become impaired to the point where we may think that having a drink will make us feel better.

I assured Dolly that attendance at meetings, working the Twelve Steps, and taking inventory each day would let her see what was bringing her closer to God and the maintenance of sobriety. If her old patterns of destructive thinking and behaviour began to surface, she was to contact her sponsor immediately – before they became ingrained and could set the stage for relapse.

Since Dolly read her Bible daily, she was encouraged to dwell on the passages that expressed the wisdom of living one day at a time under divine protection. I also recommended that she read the words as if Jesus were speaking to her personally. For instance, the passage from Isaiah 43:4-5 could be read like this: "Dolly, you are precious in my sight, and honoured, and I love you…. Do not fear, for I am with you."

Though I have not seen Dolly for a number of years, I remember her parting words. She referred to herself as the prodigal daughter who once was lost, but now is found; who once was dead, but now has come to life. These words, taken from Scripture, capture the essence of transformation and rebirth, of being "born again."

Create in me a clean heart, O God,
and put a new and right spirit within me.

Psalm 51:10

Step Eight

*Made a list of all persons we had harmed,
and became willing to make amends to them all.*

Step Nine

*Made direct amends to such people wherever
possible, except when to do so would injure
them or others.*

Steps Eight and Nine are action steps devoted to the restoration of right relationships. Although we may express sorrow for our misdeeds, repentance, forgiveness and reconciliation require much more. Mouthing the words "I'm sorry" isn't enough. These steps demand humility and action, the requisites for a radical change of heart, which will transform our attitudes and behaviours.

Steps Eight and Nine are also referred to as the "amends" steps. We are all required to make amends. We have to acknowledge the pain we have caused others through insensitivity, wilfulness, pride, selfishness or mean-spiritedness, and we must make restitution where possible and appropriate. Although truth can be a great healer, it can also wound and destroy if not told with compassion. There are definitely instances where disclosure would not be wise, because the consequences could be detrimental to all involved. For instance, if we have engaged in extramarital affairs, it would not be prudent to divulge this devastating news to our unsuspecting spouses without warning. It would be wiser – and more humane – to consult with a clergy person or counsellor who could evaluate the situation and help us decide on a favourable approach to resolve this difficult situation.

Even though we are now ready to make amends to those we have harmed, they may reject our apologies. Nonetheless, our part is to start the reconciliation process, carry it through and relinquish the outcome to God.

Although it is important to make amends to others, it is also of primary importance that we make amends to ourselves. This could be difficult if we are overcome with shame, guilt, low self-esteem and the sense that we are unworthy of God's love and forgiveness. We must shed this vindictive view that we have created to support our disparaging self-image, and learn to measure our worth instead through God's everlasting love and acceptance. "The steadfast love of the LORD never ceases, his mercies never come to an end; they are new every morning; great is your faithfulness." (Lamentations 3:22-23)

Learning to Cherish Ourselves

Self-love is not to be equated with selfishness or self-obsession. It means bestowing upon ourselves the same love and consideration that we bestow upon others. Self-love enables us to see our goodness. Women's lack of self-love manifests itself in sins of omission. How many times have we discounted or ignored our creative abilities or unexplored talents because of other commitments or just plain inertia? I knew a woman who generously volunteered her time and skills with numerous groups. Because she had artistic talent, her family and friends encouraged her to take art lessons. She, too, realized that she was gifted, but she always had reasons why she could not attend classes. The reasons usually revolved around family responsibilities, which seemed legitimate at the time. Years later, the former obstacles no longer existed but new excuses prevailed. It takes courage to leave comfortable routines and safe havens to venture onto new paths. For whatever reason, this woman was not ready to take the challenge. This story may resonate with many who have put aside their hopes and dreams for another day, only to find that time has slipped by and that special day never arrives.

Fortunately, there are women who are trying new ventures. At one 55+ club, women from the ages of fifty-five to eighty-five participate in activities ranging from dance and fitness to computer, art and writing classes. They are a dynamic group, and their spirit of enthusiasm and vitality provides compelling evidence that it is never too late to explore new horizons and follow your dreams.

In the Bible, we see Jesus as a guest at the home of Martha and Mary. Martha is distracted by all the preparations and is annoyed that Mary is listening to Jesus instead of helping her. When Martha implores Jesus to tell Mary to help her, he replies: "Martha, Martha, you are worried and distracted by many things; there is need of only one thing. Mary has chosen the better part, which will not be taken away from her." (Luke 10:38-42) This is not to say that our household tasks are not important, but rather that from time to time our priorities will be challenged. The question then becomes this: What is more important, replenishing our physical needs or our spiritual needs? Our objective in recovery is to live a balanced lifestyle that integrates both spiritual and corporal aspects into our daily routines.

The truth is that if we are to have a proper relationship with God, we must be both a Mary and a Martha. We must give our attention to God in the same way that Mary gave her attention to Jesus. This means taking time to rearrange our priorities in order to devote time to prayer and meditation. We are still called upon to be doers who participate in our daily responsibilities, but when we place God first, even mundane chores can bring a sense of satisfaction and fulfillment.

Another area that illustrates women's lack of self-love is manifested in our sexuality. When we have not established healthy or appropriate boundaries, the consequences may have been disastrous. If we continually try to fill the void in our lives with numerous, superficial relationships, the ultimate result is more emotional pain: we are left feeling empty, used, ashamed and unfulfilled. This is not only spiritually devastating but physically risky, as we may become pregnant or contract sexually transmitted diseases.

In his book *Addiction and Grace*, Gerald May tells us that addiction can bring us to our knees. This is especially evident when addiction, combined with extramarital sex, results in the destruction of our marriages. I have listened to the tragic and painful stories of many husbands and wives who have yielded to the lure of infidelity, and lost more than they ever could have imagined.

One man told me that he had been married for thirty years when he became bored and dissatisfied with his marriage. During this period, he met a young woman who made him feel alive again. He became so enamoured and obsessed with her that he quickly divorced his wife in order to marry his new love. They had not been married long, however, when he discovered that the honeymoon was over. She suddenly lost interest in him sexually; once the physical part of the relationship was gone, there was not much left.

Because of this relationship, he had lost the respect of his children. Although he was invited to his youngest son's wedding, he was not seated at the head table as father of the groom. When he went home that evening, he cried. For the first time, he realized how much he had given up, and how his selfish, immature actions had severed family ties.

This man told me that he would advise others who were contemplating or involved in affairs to try and restore their marriages instead. "Some marriages can't be saved, but at least you will know you tried. They won't listen, though; I know I didn't. My friends tried to talk to me, but I was so blinded by the excitement of the moment that I didn't think about anything else. I wish I could turn back the clock and change the outcome. I can't, but I can tell you from experience, the price was too high."

Responsible Choices

We have to make responsible decisions about our intimate relationships. A loving commitment that unites body, mind and spirit can be a sacred experience that satisfies our need for unity. Cherishing our sexuality and making choices that honour our integrity will help us carry out such a commitment.

Our lack of self-love also expresses itself in the compulsive behaviours of overeating, undereating, bingeing and purging. When we deny or repress our uncomfortable feelings and use food to mask our pain, we are abusing ourselves. Compulsive eating, bulimia and anorexia will eventually damage our bodies, so we need to find healthier ways to reduce stress.

In Step Three, I spoke about the profound sense of shame, defilement and spiritual confusion that victims of sexual abuse have experienced. What I have noticed about these women is that many do not act out their anger and rage at their perpetrators, but rather turn it inward in the form of self-punishment. In many cases, this is played out in eating disorders and chemical dependency.

A woman named Beth told me that when she entered puberty, her older brother began to abuse her sexually. As he was fondling her, he would tell her how beautiful and sensuous her body had become. She somehow felt it was her fault that she had become desirable and a source of temptation to him. In order to combat his advances she began to overeat. Once she became fat, he lost interest in her, and she saw her obesity as a godsend. Today, Beth has difficulty accepting compliments from men and blushes easily. Many people tease her about this. They see it as cute and coy, but Beth isn't being coy. Compliments bring shame and anxiety to the surface and, instead of feeling good about the attention, she is haunted by past humiliations.

Anorexia nervosa can be another way to deal with sexual abuse and reduce a woman's sexual appeal. When a woman starves herself, her menstrual cycles may cease and her breasts may become smaller as her feminine body takes on the appearance of an emaciated little boy. (I should note that not all women who suffer from eating disorders have been sexually abused, but there is always an emotional component involved.)

People may wonder why anyone would want to mar or destroy her body through overeating or starvation, but when we try to imagine the horror a person must endure as her body is overpowered and subjected to the invasion of another, we can view eating disorders from a different perspective. They may appear to be a way of numbing feelings or taking control of life once again. As women, we may tell ourselves that while we may have been powerless to stop the abuse, we can control food intake. We can choose to eat or refuse to put food into our mouths. In order to be healthy, we must learn to use food for nourishment and not as a means of self-destruction.

Eating disorders are complex. We may need a therapist's help to face our emotional needs and come to terms with the physical dangers involved in both compulsive eating and self-starvation.

As we can see, amends apply not only to others but to ourselves as well. Our amends begin the reconciliation process. Our God wants us to love ourselves, to grow in self-esteem and to embrace our gifts. As we let go of alienation and despair, we encounter oneness with God, others and ourselves. It is in reconciling that we experience divine grace and are blessed with forgiveness, as we forgive others.

Search me, O God, and know my heart;
   test me and know my thoughts.
See if there is any wicked way in me,
   and lead me in the way everlasting.

Psalm 139:23-24

Step Ten

*Continued to take personal inventory
and when we were wrong promptly admitted it.*

Step Ten is devoted to maintaining and restoring right relationships, which are vital to our ongoing recovery. The importance of a daily personal inventory cannot be stressed enough. In order to maintain a healthy spiritual life, we must be honest with God, our neighbour and ourselves in the present moment. Our spiritual life is predicated on "one day at a time."

Although we may resist this ongoing task of self-examination, our health depends on it. If we do not do a daily inventory, we will eventually fall back into old, familiar routines, and reap the consequences of our misguided, destructive attitudes and behaviours once again. We will rationalize, justify or blame others for our wrongdoings, and, like the Genesis account of Adam and Eve in the Garden of Eden, we, too, will make excuses and abdicate responsibility for our actions.

In Steps Four and Five, we looked at the importance of dealing with our anger before it hardened into resentment. Another malady that often accompanies resentment is the green-eyed monster called envy. Envy usually surfaces when we perceive others as having what we lack and would like to possess – whether it be physical beauty, popularity, talent or wealth. Envy also puts us in a competitive mode; we cannot appreciate or be happy with the success of others because we feel that their gifts diminish us in some way. In other words, we feel deprived. Opportunities and possessions have somehow eluded us and so we covet our neighbour's goods.

This spiritual issue is exemplified in Genesis 29:31-35 and 30:1, where we see the childless Rachel envying Leah, who had given birth to four sons, and in Genesis 37:3-28, when Joseph's brothers sold him to the Ishmaelites because they resented the fact that their father favoured Joseph. In Matthew 27:18, it is clear that Pontius Pilate was aware that Jesus was delivered to him for crucifixion due to the chief priests' envy.

When envy rears its ugly head, it can manifest itself in malicious remarks that are intended to undermine another's character, or in extreme forms such as the violence extended to Jesus and Joseph. Whatever forms it takes, it is a destructive power that replaces love and damages relationships. "For where there is envy and selfish ambition, there will also be disorder and wickedness of every kind." (James 3:16)

When we are overcome by envy, we have forgotten our true identity as children of God, and that we are "fearfully and wonderfully made." (Psalm 139:14) While it is true that each of us has different gifts and abilities, by the standards of God one is not more important than another. It is our values that are out of sync; we tend to believe that some gifts are superior to others. In 1 Corinthians 12:4-31, Paul talks about the variety of spiritual gifts present in the community and uses the body as an analogy to clarify how our diversity emanates from one God. It is important that our personal inventories list our strengths and assets, so we can appreciate our unique talents and blessings. We must focus on internal qualities instead of judging ourselves strictly by external appearances.

Step Ten invites us to be vigilant and honest with ourselves, because old temptations and unrecognized compulsive habits can be deeply entrenched and difficult to eradicate. If we do not acknowledge our failures, we will stay trapped in self-delusion. However, if we take time each day to look at our indiscretions, as well as at the anger, pain, fear and grief residing within us, we will open our hearts to the awareness needed for healing and acceptance. As the Bible says, "And you will know the truth, and the truth will make you free." (John 8:32)

Although recognizing and acknowledging our shortcomings are vital to our recovery, again, more is required. We must also be willing to change negative attitudes and behaviours in order for progress and transformation to occur. We must die to selfish and wilful desires that are barriers to an abundant life. "Very truly, I tell you, unless a grain of wheat falls into the earth and dies, it remains just a single grain; but if it dies, it bears much fruit." (John 12:24)

Since fear has been one of my shortcomings, I have examined the role it has played in my life. Fear can be a positive force when it signals impending danger that could lead to injury or death. On the other hand, fear that is the result of insecurity is another matter. In my case, self-imposed fear has caused me unnecessary anxiety and lost opportunities. Whenever an occasion arose that could enhance my life or career, the old negative tapes would reactivate and stir up my fear of failure, ridicule or rejection.

I know that fearful thoughts will continue to surface as I deepen my vision and expand my horizons. If I allow them to dominate my life and affect my decisions, I will remain trapped and immobilized. To reduce fear, I must constantly confront and respond to it in positive ways. I have to let go of thoughts that have caused me to substitute fear for faith. I have chosen to place my trust in God and believe in these words, which open the door to spiritual freedom: "Fear knocked at the door – Faith answered and lo, there was no one there."

God knows our limitations and does not expect us to be perfect or to live up to impossible ideals. We are fallible human beings who struggle constantly with our imperfections. Rather than viewing our inadequacies, limitations and frustrations in terms of weakness and failure, we can see them in terms of God's grace. The fact that God continues to work through wounded humanity proves that the divine power that emanates through us is truly a miracle. The gospel message has been communicated throughout the centuries despite the personal limitations of the messengers. Biblical records show that personal vulnerability and feelings of inadequacy have been powerful instruments in revealing the presence of God to the people.

In the Old Testament, Moses felt utterly incapable of being the spokesperson for the chosen people. He said to God: "Who am I that I should go to Pharaoh, and bring the Israelites out of Egypt?" (Exodus 3:11) The New Testament depicts Paul as being very aware of his weaknesses and limitations. Listen to what he has to say: "And I came to you in weakness and in fear and in much trembling. My speech and my proclamation were not with plausible words of wisdom, but with a demonstration of the Spirit and of power, so that your faith might rest not on human wisdom but on the power of God." (1 Corinthians 2:3-5) Paul was able to see that it was through his human weakness that he experienced the strength of God. God works through the vulnerability and helplessness of those who are willing to surrender to this life-sustaining power and become instruments for the Spirit of God.

Sometimes it is difficult to look back on our lives prior to recovery, but we do this in order to learn from our mistakes and grow spiritually. Paul did not deny his shadow side; he had persecuted Christ before becoming Christ's ambassador. (1 Corinthians 15:9) We, too, must never deny or ignore the shadow side of our personalities or we will lose a part of our being that needs the attention and the healing power of God's divine grace. When we expose our shadow side to the light, we must be gentle with ourselves, and grateful for the grace that frees us from feeling unworthy. We now treat ourselves as God would treat us: with unconditional love, compassion, respect and understanding. "I have loved you with an everlasting love: therefore I have continued my faithfulness to you." (Jeremiah 31:3)

I pray that the God of our Lord Jesus Christ, the Father of glory, may give you a spirit of wisdom and revelation as you come to know him, so that, with the eyes of your heart enlightened, you may know what is the hope to which he has called you, what are the riches of his glorious inheritance among the saints, and what is the immeasurable greatness of his power for us who believe, according to the working of his great power.

Ephesians 1:17-19

Step Eleven

Sought through prayer and meditation to improve our conscious contact with God as we understood Him, praying only for knowledge of His will for us and the power to carry that out.

In Step Eleven we have, again, a call to faith, because prayer and meditation require us to let go of control and put our complete trust in God. These are ways to commune with God, enrich our faith and nourish our impoverished souls so that we can grow in spiritual maturity.

Prayer and meditation can bring about profound changes in our lives. When we ask for guidance and enlightenment, we become receptive to the wisdom of God. When we surrender to God's will, we become wiser and better – a new creation. "So if anyone is in Christ, there is a new creation: everything old has passed away; see, everything has become new!" (2 Corinthians 5:17)

When we pray, we do not have to assail God with a barrage of words. The power of prayer does not depend on

81

our verbal expertise but rather on God, who listens to our prayers. It is God, not us, who does the work. I have seen people healed, individuals protected and guided in the midst of dangerous and difficult situations, and broken relationships mended as a result of prayer. The answer to our prayers may not always take the form we would like. Nonetheless, we must be totally receptive to the will of God, for we know we will be given what we really need, and our problems will be resolved with our best interests at heart.

If we do not pray and meditate daily, we are in jeopardy of undermining our spiritual foundation. "Unless the LORD builds the house, those who build it labour in vain." (Psalm 127:1) Prayer can encompass many forms: praise, thanksgiving, worship, invocation, intercessory, and scriptural readings. Prayer can also be expressed through music, art, poetry, guided imagery, dream work and journalling, and in physical expressions such as walking and dancing. We need to be free and spontaneous in developing methods that enhance our spirituality.

Meditation or contemplative prayer allows us to discern and become receptive to the still voice within each of us. "Be still, and know that I am God!" (Psalm 46:10) It is in the silence and solitude of meditation that we surrender to divine mystery and connect with the kingdom of God in the here and now. "The kingdom of God does not come visibly, nor will people say, 'Here it is,' or 'There it is,' because the kingdom of God is within you." (Luke 17:20-21 NIV)

Meditation is best done in a setting that is free of distractions, a place where our busy minds have a chance to become peaceful and responsive to the spirit within. John Main, a Benedictine monk, suggests that we sit in an upright position; once our breathing becomes calm and regular, we begin the mantra: *Maranatha.* This is an ancient Aramaic prayer that means "Come, Lord Jesus." Ma-ra-na-tha is said with the stress on each of the four syllables, for twenty or thirty minutes, twice daily. The Lord's Prayer is also a rich resource for contemplation when it is meditated on rather than rattled off by rote. Initially, meditation is difficult to do because we are deluged by our busy thoughts, but it does become easier with patience and practice.

Many women lead hectic lives that involve the responsibilities of marriage, motherhood, careers and other activities. The thought of another commitment can seem overwhelming, but it is precisely because our lifestyles deplete us emotionally, spiritually and physically that prayer and meditation should become an integral part of our daily routine. When we are willing to spend time with God each day, we learn to quiet our minds and bodies, and our serenity and energy are restored. Mother Teresa of Calcutta once said that the more time she spent in prayer and meditation, the more strength she was given to accomplish her ministry with the sick and dying.

It is through prayer and meditation that we "improve our conscious contact with God," as Step Eleven puts it. Mistaking our egos or wilful minds for the voice of the Holy Spirit can cause problems, but St. Paul gives clear, concise instructions on discernment. The renewal and transformation he speaks of in Ephesians 4:22-32, Romans 12:2 and Colossians 1:9-14 are always at one with the Spirit of God. Paul also informs us of the thoughts we must cultivate in order for renewal to occur. "Whatever is true, whatever is honourable, whatever is just, whatever is pure, whatever is pleasing, whatever is commendable, if there is any excellence and if there is anything worthy of praise, think about these things." (Philippians 4:8)

Because spiritual insights do not function through logic, our intuitive knowing and inspiration are often dismissed or considered strange and irrational by a society that extols the scientific and analytical mindset. In reviewing our past, we may become aware of times when we have neglected or refused to listen to our intuition and suffered the consequences. When we acknowledge this deeper knowing, which does not often make sense at the time, we will be rewarded. Events and opportunities will arise that we never thought possible, and we will be given the wisdom and resources needed to carry out God's plan in our lives.

I have found dream work to be a valuable tool for getting in touch with aspects of myself that I have repressed or denied. As a source of wisdom and inner truth, the symbolic language of dreams can yield valuable and powerful insights. When unconscious messages are brought to our conscious awareness, they can enlighten us in problem-solving.

The Bible tells many stories of dreams being used for instructional purposes, and of major decisions made solely on the premise of dreams. On three occasions in the Gospel of Matthew, an angel appears to Joseph and gives him orders: he is to take Mary as his wife (Matthew 1:20-24), he is to flee with his family to Egypt (2:13-15), and he and his family are to return to Israel (2:19-

22). Because Joseph obeyed the orders revealed to him in his dreams, he and his family were protected and escaped unharmed.

Two dreams I had expressed my spiritual challenge. Because of the insights I acquired from this night wisdom, I was able to step out in faith.

I had been a court reporter for five years when I had to decide whether I wanted to continue with this work or pursue a new career as a hospital chaplain. The new career meant that I would eventually have to leave home and family, and move to another city in order to study. At this time, fear permeated my life and I had reservations about giving up the secure and the familiar for the unknown.

One night I had a vivid dream. The dream took place in the biblical setting of Sodom and Gomorrah. Lot and his family were leaving the city and were told not to look back. Lot's wife did look back and was turned into a pillar of salt. I then heard a loud voice cry out: "Don't be like Lot's wife and look back. Keep looking forward!" In this ancient setting, a small aircraft appeared in the sky and spelled out the letters L.O.T. Again, a loud voice cried out: "Love, Obey, Trust!"

Another dream, which was more of a nightmare, was my snake dream. The snake would strike at me and then wind itself around me. I think my psyche was trying to get my attention. Psychiatrist Jean Shinoda Bolen has said that when women begin to claim their power they are likely to dream about snakes. Although the snake is a symbol of evil in Christian mythology, this is not the case in the mythology of many other cultures, where it is a symbol of change, healing, creativity, transition and self-renewal.

In light of this information, I could see there was a correlation between my two dreams. They were definitely wake-up calls. It was my responsibility to shed the old and take advantage of the new opportunity that had presented itself. I also had to slough off all the attitudes, behaviours and relationships that had hindered my growth in order to recreate myself. Like the snake, I would experience the transition period between old and new as a very vulnerable time. Because of these dreams, however, I was able to accept the challenge of a new career, plus the geographical change it entailed. I discovered that when one is willing to listen to Divine Wisdom with an open heart and mind, resources are provided for the journey. As we devote time each day to prayer and meditation, our renewed minds will become receptive to the ways of the Spirit. When we look upon prayer and meditation as a way of communicating with someone we love rather than an obligation, we will develop a personal and intimate relationship with our Creator and reap the benefits of the Spirit-filled life.

Then Jesus went about all the cities and villages, teaching in their synagogues, and proclaiming the good news of the kingdom, and curing every disease and every sickness. When he saw the crowds, he had compassion for them, because they were harassed and helpless, like sheep without a shepherd. Then he said to his disciples, "The harvest is plentiful, but the labourers are few; therefore ask the Lord of the harvest to send out labourers into his harvest."

Matthew 9:35-38

Step Twelve

Having had a spiritual awakening as the result of these steps, we tried to carry this message to alcoholics, and to practice these principles in all our affairs.

In this final step, we are invited to be faithful witnesses to the goodness of God's grace and mercy. We all need to hear how the God of our understanding delivers us from the bondage of addiction, and promises new life if we commit to the principles outlined in the Bible and the Twelve Steps.

Telling our story is an integral part of our spiritual journey, for it is through story that we share our lives with each other. As we share strengths, weaknesses, hopes and dreams, we interact with others and receive support and encouragement that is not possible in isolation. By offering and accepting empathy, compassion and solidarity, we renew our well-being and maintain hope in the midst of our struggles.

There is no greater gift than listening. In listening to the stories of others, our own experiences are mirrored back to us and we realize that we are neither unique nor alone in our suffering. We come to see that the wounds of life have left scars on all of us, and limited our ability to live life to the fullest. Our stories bring us to spiritual enlightenment as we learn that God cares and shares in our recovery. Story is witness to the power of God's love manifested in the community of recovering people. "Let us hold unswervingly to the hope we profess, for he who promised is faithful. And let us consider how we may spur one another on toward love and good deeds. Let us not give up meeting together, as some are in the habit of doing, but let us encourage one another…." (Hebrews 10:23-25 NIV)

Whether our affiliation is with a Twelve Step group, a church, or both, we are a community of faith. The Bible and the Twelve Step principles empower us and set us free. "I am the LORD your God, who brought you out of the land of Egypt, out of the house of slavery: you shall have no other gods before me." (Deuteronomy 5:6-7) In concrete terms, we are shown how the sacred is experienced in community as we are blessed and released from addictive slavery and restored to wholeness. We are all witnesses to the fact that if we are receptive to God's will, we can be transformed. The promises in the Big Book proclaim our freedom and rebirth.

We are going to know a new freedom and a new happiness. We will not regret the past nor wish to shut the door on it. We will comprehend the word serenity and we will know peace. No matter how far down the scale we have gone, we will see how our experience can benefit others. That feeling of uselessness and self-pity will disappear. We will lose interest in selfish things and gain interest in our fellows. Self-seeking will slip away. Our whole attitude and outlook upon life will change. Fear of people and of economic insecurity will leave us. We will intuitively know how to handle situations which used to baffle us. We will suddenly realize that God is doing for us what we could not do for ourselves.[8]

As we are transformed and become a new creation, we are blessed with the fruits of the spirit that Paul describes: "love, joy, peace, patience, kindness, generosity, faithfulness, gentleness and self-control." (Galatians 5:22-23)

The promises contained in both the Big Book and Paul's letter to the Galatians are no longer mere words: we have experienced them. We are reborn; we are a new creation; we are living the miracle of recovery. We are now asked to carry this good news to others who are still in bondage and suffering in the throes of addiction.

Although I have talked about the benefits we can obtain if we follow the principles of recovery, I want to clarify that even if we are diligent in applying them to our daily lives, we are not guaranteed a pain-free existence. Sorrow and adversity are part of the human condition, and our tribulations and disappointments can make our spirits weary. We may even question God's love and faithfulness. We may ask: "Why do I have to suffer so much when I have tried to be a good person?" There is no easy answer to this difficult question. I have come to realize that "Why?" is not a helpful question. Often, what we need in the midst of painful experiences is not so much a suitable answer but rather a sustaining faith and the ability to endure hardships without emotional or spiritual bitterness. Rather than asking "Why?" I now ask what I can learn from loss and adversity, and where I can sense the presence of God amidst the suffering.

In the past few years, I have had to cope with a number of grief issues and health problems in my personal life. I wondered how I could turn my pain, fatigue and discouragement into something constructive, creative and life-giving. It was through this difficult time that my trust in God deepened and I discovered an inner strength that I did not know I possessed. I then thought of all the women I had ministered to over the years, through counselling and listening to Fifth Steps; out of our collective stories, this book came into being.

The Book of Job addresses the problem of suffering in great detail; Job comes to the realization that his suffering gave him wisdom and a new understanding of God (Job 42:2-6). Suffering can be a great teacher if we are willing to embrace its lessons. When we come to understand the importance of fidelity, patience, courage, empathy and compassion in times of difficulty and uncertainty, we will begin to sense the presence of God amidst the chaos.

Allan is a man who, like Job, accepted the lessons of suffering with courage and dignity. At the age of forty-seven he had to take early retirement due to complications arising from his diabetes. Many of us would be upset and bitter if our careers ended in such a way, and our existence became dependent on a dialysis machine.

To my surprise, Allan told me that despite all he has lost, he has never been more peaceful or content. With a profound faith, which he expressed in simple terms, he shared the essence of his being. He said that through the strain and pressure of his illness, he has learned to accept himself exactly as he is. "What you see is what you get. This is what I have been given, and this is where I am meant to be, whether I like it or not. You learn from adversity. If I focus on the negative, I will be miserable and that would be dumb."

A friend once sent me a card that read: "Joy is not the absence of suffering but the presence of God." Allan lives that message. Even though his body is afflicted by disease, he refuses to let his spirit be touched by despair.

Allan embraced the Roman Catholic faith shortly before his retirement. He told me he does not know how he would have coped had he not experienced the comfort of God. "When I can't do it anymore, God takes over." Needless to say, Allan is an inspiration to many as he exemplifies "the peace of God, which surpasses all understanding." (Philippians 4:7)

The Bible assures us that God does not forsake us in times of heartache and tribulation. When we call upon God for help, we will be blessed with inner strength, joy, peace and serenity. "Then you shall call, and the LORD will answer; you shall cry for help, and he will say, Here I am." (Isaiah 58:9)

Jesus suffered, too. He experienced loneliness, sorrow, rejection and betrayal in his agony in the garden, but he did not advocate suffering for suffering's sake. He wished the cup to be taken from him. "My Father, if it is possible, let this cup pass from me; yet not what I want but what you want." (Matthew 26:39) God fully understands our suffering, and promises to be with us always: "I will never leave you or forsake you." (Hebrews 13:5)

Most of us have endured a variety of losses and afflictions in our lives, so we know how vital the support of others is to our well-being. Grief that is shared becomes less. Even in our deepest sorrow, we know that we are not alone, as God's fidelity is experienced in the empathy and encouragement of our community. Twelve Step groups are dwelling places for the oppressed and downtrodden. They facilitate healing amidst the human conditions of sadness, estrangement and despair.

The Bible and the Twelve Step principles offer us hope and strength as we continue our lifelong commitment to recovery and transformation. They entail a spiritual process based on the precepts of love, surrender, conversion, redemption and reconciliation, which in turn bring about a new relationship with God, ourselves and our neighbour.

I invite you to join this spiritual journey so that you, too, can participate in the gift of recovery, quench your spiritual thirst, and be a witness to the miracle of new beginnings. "The Spirit and the bride say, 'Come.' And let everyone who hears say, 'Come.' And let everyone who is thirsty come. Let anyone who wishes take the water of life as a gift." (Revelation 22:17)

Part Two

Words of Consolation

The Sermon on the Mount: The Beatitudes

"Blessed are the poor in spirit, for theirs is the kingdom of heaven.

Blessed are those who mourn, for they will be comforted.

Blessed are the meek, for they will inherit the earth.

Blessed are those who hunger and thirst for righteousness, for they will be filled.

Blessed are the merciful, for they will receive mercy.

Blessed are the pure in heart, for they will see God.

Blessed are the peacemakers, for they will be called children of God.

Blessed are those who are persecuted for righteousness' sake, for theirs is the kingdom of heaven.

Blessed are you when people revile you and persecute you and utter all kinds of evil against you falsely on my account. Rejoice and be glad, for your reward is great in heaven, for in the same way they persecuted the prophets who were before you."

Matthew 5:3-12

The Lord's Prayer

Our Father in heaven,
hallowed be your name.
Your kingdom come.
Your will be done,
    on earth as it is in heaven.
Give us this day our daily bread.
And forgive us our debts,
    as we also have forgiven our debtors.
And do not bring us to the time of trial,
    but rescue us from the evil one.

Matthew 6:9-13

Step One

We admitted we were powerless over alcohol —
that our lives had become unmanageable.

My heart is in anguish within me,
    the terrors of death have fallen upon me.
Fear and trembling come upon me,
    and horror overwhelms me.
And I say, "O that I had wings like a dove!
    I would fly away and be at rest;
    truly, I would flee far away;
I would lodge in the wilderness;
I would hurry to find a shelter for myself
    from the raging wind and tempest."

Psalm 55:4-8

Who has woe? Who has sorrow?
    Who has strife? Who has complaining?
Who has wounds without cause?
    Who has redness of eyes?
Those who linger late over wine,
    those who keep trying mixed wines.
Do not look at wine when it is red,
    when it sparkles in the cup
    and goes down smoothly.
At the last it bites like a serpent,
    and stings like an adder.
Your eyes will see strange things,
    and your mind utter perverse things.
You will be like one who lies down
    in the midst of the sea,
    like one who lies on the top of a mast.
"They struck me," you will say, "but I was not hurt;
    they beat me, but I did not feel it.
When shall I awake?
    I will seek another drink."

Proverbs 23:29-35

Be careful then how you live, not as unwise people but as wise, making the most of the time,
because the days are evil. So do not be foolish,
but understand what the will of the Lord is. Do
not get drunk with wine, for that is debauchery;
but be filled with the Spirit....

Ephesians 5:15-18

Step Two

Came to believe that a Power greater than
ourselves could restore us to sanity.

Turn to me and be gracious to me,
    for I am lonely and afflicted.
Relieve the troubles of my heart,
    and bring me out of my distress.
Consider my affliction and my trouble,
    and forgive all my sins.

Consider how many are my foes,
    and with what violent hatred they hate me.
O guard my life, and deliver me;
    do not let me be put to shame,
    for I take refuge in you.
May integrity and uprightness preserve me,
    for I wait for you.

Psalm 25:16-21

Be gracious to me, O LORD, for I am in distress;
    my eye wastes away from grief,
    my soul and body also.
For my life is spent with sorrow,
    and my years with sighing;
my strength fails because of my misery,
    and my bones waste away.

I am the scorn of all my adversaries,
    a horror to my neighbours,
an object of dread to my acquaintances;
    those who see me in the street flee from me.
I have passed out of mind like one who is dead;
    I have become like a broken vessel.
For I hear the whispering of many –
    terror all around!– …

Psalm 31:9-13

I will instruct you and teach you
    the way you should go;
    I will counsel you with my eye upon you.
Do not be like a horse or a mule,
    without understanding,
    whose temper must be curbed with bit and bridle,
    else it will not stay near you.

Psalm 32:8-9

I waited patiently for the LORD;
    he inclined to me and heard my cry.
He drew me up from the desolate pit,
    out of the miry bog,

and set my feet upon a rock,
    making my steps secure.
He put a new song in my mouth,
    a song of praise to our God.
Many will see and fear,
    and put their trust in the LORD.

Happy are those who make
    the LORD their trust,
who do not turn to the proud,
    to those who go astray after false gods.
                                        Psalm 40:1-4

God is our refuge and strength,
    a very present help in trouble.
Therefore we will not fear,
    though the earth should change,
    though the mountains shake
    in the heart of the sea;
though its waters roar and foam,
    though the mountains tremble with its tumult.
                                        Psalm 46:1-3

Be merciful to me, O God, be merciful to me,
    for in you my soul takes refuge;
in the shadow of your wings I will take refuge,
    until the destroying storms pass by.
                                        Psalm 57:1

I will repay you for the years
    that the swarming locust has eaten,
the hopper, the destroyer, and the cutter,
    my great army, which I sent against you.
You shall eat in plenty and be satisfied,
    and praise the name of the LORD your God,
    who has dealt wondrously with you.
And my people shall never again be put to shame.
You shall know that I am in the midst of Israel,
    and that I, the LORD, am your God
    and there is no other.
And my people shall never again
    be put to shame.

Joel 2:25-27

Let us therefore approach the throne of grace
with boldness, so that we may receive mercy and
find grace to help in time of need.

Hebrews 4:16

Step Three

Made a decision to turn our will and our lives
over to the care of God as we understood Him.

Trust in the LORD, and do good;
  so you will live in the land, and enjoy security.
Take delight in the LORD,
  and he will give you the desires of your heart.
Psalm 37:3-4

Our steps are made firm by the LORD,
  when he delights in our way;
though we stumble, we shall not fall headlong,
  for the LORD holds us by the hand.
Psalm 37:23-24

I lift up my eyes to the hills –
  from where will my help come?
My help comes from the LORD,
  who made heaven and earth.

He will not let your foot be moved;
   he who keeps you will not slumber.
He who keeps Israel
   will neither slumber nor sleep.

The LORD is your keeper;
   the LORD is your shade at your right hand.
The sun shall not strike you by day,
   nor the moon by night.

The LORD will keep you from all evil;
   he will keep your life.
The LORD will keep
   your going out and your coming in
   from this time on and forevermore.

Psalm 121:1-8

Happy is everyone who fears the LORD,
   who walks in his ways.
You shall eat the fruit of the labour of your hands;
   you shall be happy,
   and it shall go well with you.

Psalm 128:1-2

Teach me to do your will,
   for you are my God.
Let your good spirit lead me
   on a level path.

Psalm 143:10

The LORD upholds all who are falling,
   and raises up all who are bowed down.
The eyes of all look to you,
   and you give them their food in due season.

You open your hand,
>   satisfying the desire of every living thing.
The LORD is just in all his ways,
>   and kind in all his doings.
The LORD is near to all who call on him,
>   to all who call on him in truth.

Psalm 145:14-18

The LORD builds up Jerusalem;
>   he gathers the outcasts of Israel.
He heals the brokenhearted,
>   and binds up their wounds.

Psalm 147:2-3

Trust in the LORD with all your heart,
>   and do not rely on your own insight.
In all your ways acknowledge him,
>   and he will make straight your paths.

Proverbs 3:5-6

For I will restore health to you,
>   and your wounds I will heal, says the LORD,
because they have called you an outcast:
>   "It is Zion; no one cares for her!"

Jeremiah 30:17

"Come to me, all you that are weary and are carrying heavy burdens, and I will give you rest. Take my yoke upon you, and learn from me; for I am gentle and humble in heart, and you will find rest for your souls. For my yoke is easy, and my burden is light."

Matthew 11:28-30

If I speak in the tongues of mortals and of angels, but do not have love, I am a noisy gong or a clanging cymbal. And if I have prophetic powers, and understand all mysteries and all knowledge, and if I have all faith, so as to remove mountains, but do not have love, I am nothing. If I give away all my possessions, and if I hand over my body so that I may boast, but do not have love, I gain nothing.

Love is patient; love is kind; love is not envious or boastful or arrogant or rude. It does not insist on its own way; it is not irritable or resentful; it does not rejoice in wrongdoing, but rejoices in the truth. It bears all things, believes all things, hopes all things, endures all things.

Love never ends. But as for prophecies, they will come to an end; as for tongues, they will cease; as for knowledge, it will come to an end. For we know only in part, and we prophesy only in part; but when the complete comes, the partial will come to an end. When I was a child, I spoke like a child, I thought like a child, I reasoned like a child; when I became an adult, I put an end to childish ways. For now we see in a mirror, dimly, but then we will see face to face. Now I know only in part; then I will know fully, even as I have been fully known. And now faith, hope, and love abide, these three; and the greatest of these is love.

1 Corinthians 13:1-13

The Wisdom Tradition

Get wisdom; get insight: do not forget,
    nor turn away
    from the words of my mouth.
Do not forsake her, and she will keep you;
    love her, and she will guard you.
The beginning of wisdom is this: Get wisdom,
    and whatever else you get, get insight.
Prize her highly, and she will exalt you;
    she will honour you if you embrace her.
She will place on your head a fair garland;
    she will bestow on you a beautiful crown.

Proverbs 4:5-9

The LORD created me at the beginning of his work,
    the first of his acts of long ago.
Ages ago I was set up,
    at the first, before the beginning of the earth.
When there were no depths I was brought forth,
    when there were no springs abounding
    with water…
When he established the heavens, I was there,
    when he drew a circle on the face of the deep,
when he made firm the skies above,
    when he established the fountains of the deep,
when he assigned to the sea its limit,
    so that the waters might not transgress his
    command,
when he marked out the foundations of the earth,
    then I was beside him, like a master worker,

and I was daily his delight,
    rejoicing before him always,
rejoicing in his inhabited world
    and delighting in the human race.

Proverbs 8:22-31

And now, my children, listen to me:
    happy are those who keep my ways.
Hear instruction and be wise,
    and do not neglect it.
Happy is the one who listens to me,
    watching daily at my gates,
    waiting beside my doors.
For whoever finds me finds life
    and obtains favour from the LORD;
but those who miss me injure themselves;
    all who hate me love death.

Proverbs 8:32-36

Feminine Images of God

As an eagle stirs up its nest,
    and hovers over its young;
as it spreads its wings, takes them up,
    and bears them aloft on its pinions...

Deuteronomy 32:11

You were unmindful of the Rock that bore you;
    you forgot the God who gave you birth.

Deuteronomy 32:18

From whose womb did the ice come forth,
    and who has given birth to the hoarfrost of
  heaven?

Job 38:29

He will feed his flock like a shepherd;
    he will gather the lambs in his arms,
and carry them in his bosom,
    and gently lead the mother sheep.

Isaiah 40:11

Rejoice with Jerusalem, and be glad for her,
    all you who love her;
rejoice with her in joy,
    all you who mourn over her –
that you may nurse and be satisfied
    from her consoling breast;
that you may drink deeply with delight
    from her glorious bosom....
As a mother comforts her child,
    so I will comfort you;
    you shall be comforted in Jerusalem.

Isaiah 66:10-11, 13

Yet it was I who taught Ephraim to walk,
    I took them up in my arms;
    but they did not know that I healed them.
I led them with cords of human kindness,
    with bands of love.
I was to them like those
    who lift infants to their cheeks.
    I bent down to them and fed them.

Hosea 11:3-4

I will fall upon them like a bear robbed of her cubs.

Hosea 13:8

And again he said, "To what should I compare the kingdom of God? It is like yeast that a woman took and mixed in with three measures of flour until all of it was leavened."

Luke 13:20-21

"Jerusalem, Jerusalem, the city that kills the prophets and stones those who are sent to it! How often have I desired to gather your children together as a hen gathers her brood under her wings, and you were not willing!"

Luke 13:34

"Or what woman having ten silver coins, if she loses one of them, does not light a lamp, sweep the house, and search carefully until she finds it? When she has found it, she calls together her friends and neighbours, saying, 'Rejoice with me, for I have found the coin that I had lost.' Just so, I tell you, there is joy in the presence of the angels of God over one sinner who repents."

Luke 15:8-10

Step Four

Made a searching and fearless moral inventory of ourselves.

Step Five

Admitted to God, to ourselves and to another human being the exact nature of our wrongs.

> Then I acknowledged my sin to you,
>   and I did not hide my iniquity;
> I said, "I will confess my transgressions to the LORD,"
>   and you forgave the guilt of my sin.
>
> *Psalm 32:5*

The people who walked in darkness
    have seen a great light;
those who lived in a land of deep darkness –
    on them light has shined.

Isaiah 9:2

So then, putting away falsehood, let all of us speak the truth to our neighbours, for we are members of one another. Be angry but do not sin; do not let the sun go down on your anger...

Ephesians 4:25-26

For once you were darkness, but now in the Lord you are light. Live as children of light – for the fruit of the light is found in all that is good and right and true. Try to find out what is pleasing to the Lord. Take no part in the unfruitful works of darkness, but instead expose them...for everything that becomes visible is light. Therefore it says,
    "Sleeper, awake!
    Rise from the dead,
    and Christ will shine on you."

Ephesians 5:8-14

If we say that we have no sin, we deceive ourselves, and the truth is not in us. If we confess our sins, he who is faithful and just will forgive us our sins and cleanse us from all unrighteousness. If we say that we have not sinned, we make him a liar, and his word is not in us.

1 John 1:8-10

Step Six

*Were entirely ready to have God remove
all these defects of character.*

Step Seven

*Humbly asked Him to remove our
shortcomings.*

Create in me a clean heart, O God,
    and put a new and right spirit within me.
Do not cast me away from your presence,
    and do not take your holy spirit from me.
Restore to me the joy of your salvation,
    and sustain in me a willing spirit.

Psalm 51:10-12

You have commanded your precepts
    to be kept diligently.
O that my ways may be steadfast
    in keeping your statutes!
Then I shall not be put to shame,
    having my eyes fixed on all your
    commandments…

How can young people keep their way pure?
    By guarding it according to your word.
With my whole heart I seek you;
    do not let me stray from your commandments.
I treasure your word in my heart,
    so that I may not sin against you.
Blessed are you, O LORD;
    teach me your statutes.
With my lips I declare
    all the ordinances of your mouth.
I delight in the way of your decrees
    as much as in all riches.
I will meditate on your precepts,
    and fix my eyes on your ways.
I will delight in your statutes;
    I will not forget your word.

Psalm 119:4-6, 9-16

No one who conceals transgressions will prosper,
    but one who confesses and forsakes them
    will obtain mercy.

Proverbs 28:13

I will sprinkle clean water upon you, and you shall be clean from all your uncleannesses, and from all your idols I will cleanse you. A new heart I will give you, and a new spirit I will put within you; and I will remove from your body the heart of stone and give you a heart of flesh. I will put my spirit within you, and make you follow my statutes and be careful to observe my ordinances. Then you shall live in the land that I gave to your ancestors; and you shall be my people, and I will be your God.

Ezekiel 36:25-28

For freedom Christ has set us free. Stand firm, therefore, and do not submit again to a yoke of slavery.

Galatians 5:1

For we ourselves were once foolish, disobedient, led astray, slaves to various passions and pleasures, passing our days in malice and envy, despicable, hating one another. But when the goodness and loving kindness of God our Saviour appeared, he saved us, not because of any works of righteousness that we had done, but according to his mercy, through the water of rebirth and renewal by the Holy Spirit. This Spirit he poured out on us richly through Jesus Christ our Saviour, so that, having been justified by his grace, we might become heirs according to the hope of eternal life.

Titus 3:3-7

Step Eight

*Made a list of all persons we had harmed,
and became willing to make amends to them all.*

Step Nine

*Made direct amends to such people wherever
possible, except when to do so would injure
them or others.*

How very good and pleasant it is
    when kindred live together in unity!
                                    Psalm 133:1

With what shall I come before the LORD,
and bow myself before God on high?…
He has told you, O mortal, what is good;
and what does the LORD require of you
but to do justice, and to love kindness,
and to walk humbly with your God?

Micah 6:6, 8

"So when you are offering your gift at the altar, if you remember that your brother or sister has something against you, leave your gift there before the altar and go; first be reconciled to your brother or sister, and then come and offer your gift."

Matthew 5:23-24

So let us not grow weary in doing what is right, for we will reap at harvest-time, if we do not give up. So then, whenever we have an opportunity, let us work for the good of all, and especially for those of the family of faith.

Galatians 6:9-10

I therefore, the prisoner in the Lord, beg you to lead a life worthy of the calling to which you have been called, with all humility and gentleness, with patience, bearing with one another in love, making every effort to maintain the unity of the Spirit in the bond of peace.

Ephesians 4:1-3

Finally, all of you, have unity of spirit, sympathy, love for one another, a tender heart, and a humble mind. Do not repay evil for evil or abuse for abuse; but, on the contrary, repay with a blessing. It is for this that you were called – that you might inherit a blessing.

1 Peter 3:8-9

Step Ten

Continued to take personal inventory and when we were wrong promptly admitted it.

Keep your heart with all vigilance,
    for from it flow the springs of life.
Put away from you crooked speech,
    and put devious talk far from you.
Let your eyes look directly forward,
    and your gaze be straight before you.
Keep straight the path of your feet,
    and all your ways will be sure.
Do not swerve to the right or to the left;
    turn your foot away from evil.

Proverbs 4:23-27

"I am the true vine, and my Father is the vinegrower. He removes every branch in me that bears no fruit. Every branch that bears fruit he prunes to make it bear more fruit. You have already been cleansed by the word that I have spoken to you. Abide in me as I abide in you. Just as the branch cannot bear fruit by itself unless it abides in the vine, neither can you unless you abide in me. I am the vine, you are the branches. Those who abide in me and I in them bear much fruit, because apart from me you can do nothing. Whoever does not abide in me is thrown away like a branch and withers; such branches are gathered, thrown into the fire, and burned. If you abide in me, and my words abide in you, ask for whatever you wish, and it will be done for you. My Father is glorified by this, that you bear much fruit and become my disciples. As the Father has loved me, so I have loved you; abide in my love. If you keep my commandments, you will abide in my love, just as I have kept my Father's commandments and abide in his love. I have said these things to you so that my joy may be in you, and that your joy may be complete."

John 15:1-11

Put to death, therefore, whatever in you is earthly: fornication, impurity, passion, evil desire, and greed (which is idolatry). On account of these the wrath of God is coming on those who are disobedient. These are the ways you also once followed, when you were living that life. But now you must get rid of all such things – anger, wrath, malice, slander, and abusive language from your mouth. Do not lie to one another, seeing that you have stripped off the old self with its practices and have clothed yourself with the new self, which is being renewed in knowledge according to the image of its creator.

Colossians 3:5-10

Now, discipline always seems painful rather than pleasant at the time, but later it yields the peaceful fruit of righteousness to those who have been trained by it.

Therefore lift your drooping hands and strengthen your weak knees, and make straight paths for your feet, so that what is lame may not be put out of joint, but rather be healed.

Hebrews 12:11-13

Step Eleven

Sought through prayer and meditation to improve our conscious contact with God as we understood Him, praying only for knowledge of His will for us and the power to carry that out.

I sought the LORD, and he answered me,
    and delivered me from all my fears.
Look to him, and be radiant;
    so your faces shall never be ashamed.

Psalm 34:4-5

You are my God, and I will give thanks to you;
    you are my God, I will extol you.
O give thanks to the LORD, for he is good,
    for his steadfast love endures forever.

Psalm 118:28-29

Hear my prayer, O LORD;
    give ear to my supplications in your
    faithfulness;
    answer me in your righteousness...

I remember the days of old,
    I think about all your deeds,
    I meditate on the works of your hands.
I stretch out my hands to you;
    my soul thirsts for you like a parched land.

Psalm 143:1, 5-6

The LORD is near to all who call on him,
    to all who call on him in truth.
He fulfills the desire of all who fear him;
    he also hears their cry, and saves them.

Psalm 145:18-19

Rejoice in the Lord always; again I will say, Rejoice. Let your gentleness be known to everyone. The Lord is near. Do not worry about anything, but in everything by prayer and supplication with thanksgiving let your requests be made known to God. And the peace of God, which surpasses all understanding, will guard your hearts and your minds in Christ Jesus.

Philippians 4:4-7

For this reason, since the day we heard it, we have not ceased praying for you and asking that you may be filled with the knowledge of God's will in all spiritual wisdom and understanding, so that you may lead lives worthy of the Lord, fully pleasing to him, as you bear fruit in every good work and as you grow in the knowledge of God. May you be made strong with all the strength that comes from his glorious power, and may you be prepared to endure everything with patience, while joyfully giving thanks to the Father, who has enabled you to share in the inheritance of the saints in the light. He has rescued us from the power of darkness and transferred us into the kingdom of his beloved Son, in whom we have redemption, the forgiveness of sins.

Colossians 1:9-14

Step Twelve

Having had a spiritual awakening as the result of these steps, we tried to carry this message to alcoholics and to practice these principles in all our affairs.

O give thanks to the LORD, call on his name,
    make known his deeds among the peoples.
Sing to him, sing praises to him;
    tell of all his wonderful works.

Psalm 105:1-2

One generation shall laud your works to another,
    and shall declare your mighty acts...

The LORD upholds all who are falling,
    and raises up all who are bowed down.
The eyes of all look to you,
    and you give them their food in due season.
You open your hand,
    satisfying the desire of every living thing.

Psalm 145:4,14-16

The spirit of the Lord GOD is upon me,
    because the LORD has anointed me;
he has sent me to bring good news to the
    oppressed,
    to bind up the brokenhearted,
to proclaim liberty to the captives,
    and release to the prisoners;
to proclaim the year of the LORD's favour,
    and the day of vengeance of our God;
    to comfort all who mourn;
to provide for those who mourn in Zion –
    to give them a garland instead of ashes,
the oil of gladness instead of mourning,
    the mantle of praise instead of a faint spirit.
They will be called oaks of righteousness,
    the planting of the LORD, to display his glory.

Isaiah 61:1-3

"You are the light of the world. A city built on a hill cannot be hid. No one after lighting a lamp puts it under the bushel basket, but on the lampstand, and it gives light to all in the house. In the same way, let your light shine before others, so that they may see your good works and give glory to your Father in heaven."

Matthew 5:14-16

Suffering

I hereby command you: Be strong and courageous; do not be frightened or dismayed, for the LORD your God is with you wherever you go.

Joshua 1:9

I say to God, my rock,
    "Why have you forgotten me?
Why must I walk about mournfully
    because the enemy oppresses me?"
As with a deadly wound in my body,
    my adversaries taunt me,
while they say to me continually,
    "Where is your God?"

Why are you cast down, O my soul,
    and why are you disquieted within me?
Hope in God; for I shall again praise him,
    my help and my God.

Psalm 42:9-11

Cast your burden on the LORD,
    and he will sustain you;
he will never permit
    the righteous to be moved.

Psalm 55:22

Those who love me, I will deliver;
    I will protect those who know my name.
When they call to me, I will answer them;
    I will be with them in trouble,
    I will rescue them and honour them.

Psalm 91:14-15

Out of my distress I called on the LORD;
    the LORD answered me and set me in a
    broad place.
With the LORD on my side I do not fear.
    What can mortals do to me?
The LORD is on my side to help me...

Psalm 118:5-7

My soul melts away for sorrow;
    strengthen me according to your word.
Put false ways far from me;
    and graciously teach me your law.

Psalm 119:28-29

The Serenity Prayer

God, grant me the Serenity
to accept the things I cannot change;
Courage to change the things I can;
and Wisdom to know the difference.

Reinhold Neibuhr

Lord, I Seek You

Lord, I seek you with all my heart,
with all the strength you have given me.
I long to understand that which I believe.

You are my only hope; please listen to me.
Do not let my weariness
lessen my desire to find you,
to see your face.

You created me in order to find you;
you gave me strength to seek you.
My strength and my weakness are in your hands:
preserve my strength, and help my weakness.
Where you have already opened the door, let
me come in;
where it is shut, open at my knocking.

Let me always remember you, love you,
meditate upon you, and pray to you,
until you restore me to your perfect pattern.

Augustine of Hippo (Confessions)

Epilogue

It has been said: "Those who bear the mark of pain are never really free; they owe a debt to the ones who still suffer.... This is your beginning."

Jesus calls us to new beginnings. Although this call will be one based on faith, it is not blind faith. When we are asked to surrender our lives to the will of God, we are assured of divine guidance and help each step of the way. The radical transformation that took place in the frightened apostles at Pentecost is a powerful testimony to this truth. The good news is that spiritual empowerment is still available to us today. One of the promises contained in the Big Book reads: "We will suddenly realize that God is doing for us what we could not do for ourselves."

Jesus invites us to enter into an intimate relationship with him. He asks us to dwell in his presence and share in his peace and joy. He encourages us to follow him and experience what he has to offer: "Come and see with the eyes of faith. Come and hear my spiritual truths. Come and taste the bread of life, the waters of renewal, which will satisfy your spiritual hunger and thirst. Let me touch you with hands that heal, and anoint you with the fragrance of forgiveness. I have come that you may have life, and have it abundantly."

I now take your hand in mine as we share our stories in a communal celebration of hope and joy. This is our beginning.

The Gift of Grace

Let the love
that God
has freely given
flow
through the wounds
of our living

Cleansing and healing
sorrow and pain
through
love
the sunrise of God
within.

Lorraine Milton

Bibliography

Alcoholics Anonymous. *Alcoholics Anonymous*. New York: AA World Services, Third Edition, 1976.

B., Dick. *The Oxford Group and Alcoholics Anonymous: An AA–Good Book Connection*. Seattle, WA: Glen Abbey Books, 1992.

B., Mel. *New Wine: The Spiritual Roots of the Twelve Step Miracle*. Center City, MN: Hazelden Foundation, 1991.

Beattie, Melody. *Codependent No More*. Center City, MN: Hazelden Foundation, 1987.

Beattie, Melody. *The Language of Letting Go*. Center City, MN: Hazelden Foundation, 1990.

Carlson, Dwight L., M.D. *Overcoming Hurts & Anger*. Eugene, OR: Harvest House Publishers, 1981.

Fisher, Bruce. *Rebuilding When Your Relationship Ends*. San Luis Obispo, CA: Impact Publishers, 1981.

Fox, Emmet. *The Sermon on the Mount: The Key to Success in Life*. New York: Collins Publishers, 1966.

Goldhor Lerner, Harriet. *The Dance of Anger*. New York: Harper & Row, 1985.

Hazelden. *In God's Care*. (Hazelden Meditation Series.) Center City, MN: Hazelden Foundation, 1996.

Hodgson, Peter C. and Robert H. King. *Christian Theology: An Introduction to Its Traditions and Tasks*. Philadelphia: Fortress Press, 1985.

Holy Bible. New International Version. Grand Rapids, MI: Zondervan Publishing, 1978.

Holy Bible. New Revised Standard Version. Grand Rapids, MI: Zondervan Publishing, 1989.

Kasl, Charlotte Davis. *Women, Sex and Addiction: A Search for Love and Power*. New York: Ticknor-Fields, 1989.

Kushner, Harold S. *When Bad Things Happen to Good People*. New York: Schoeken Books, 1981.

Macquarrie, John. *In Search of Humanity*. London: SCM Press, 1982.

Main, John. *Word into Silence*. New York/Ramsey: Paulist Press, 1981.

Matsakis, Aphrodite. *Compulsive Eaters and Relationships: Ending the Isolation*. Center City, MN: Hazelden Foundation, 1988.

May, Gerald G. *Addiction and Grace*. New York: Harper & Row, 1988.

Nakken, Craig. *The Addictive Personality: Roots, Rituals, and Recovery*. Center City, MN: Hazelden Foundation, 1988.

Norwood, Robin. *Women Who Love Too Much: When You Keep Wishing and Hoping He'll Change*. New York: Jeremy P. Tarcher, Inc./St. Martin's Press, 1985.

Osiek, Carolyn. *Beyond Anger: On Being a Feminist in the Church*. New York/Mahwah: Paulist Press, 1986.

Owen, Patricia L. *I Can See Tomorrow: A Guide for Living with Depression*. Center City, MN: Hazelden Foundation, 1995.

Peck, M. Scott. *The Road Less Traveled: A New Psychology of Love, Traditional Values and Spiritual Growth*. New York: Simon & Schuster, 1978.

Rosellini, Gayle & Mark Worden. *Of Course You're Angry: A Guide to Dealing with the Emotions of Chemical Dependence*. Center City, MN: Hazelden Foundation, 1985.

Rubin, Theodore Isaac. *The Angry Book*. New York: Collier Books, 1969.

Rupp, Joyce. *Praying Our Goodbyes*. Notre Dame, IN: Ave Maria Press, 1988.

Siegel, Bernie S. *Love, Medicine and Miracles*. New York: Harper & Row, 1986.

Stearns, Ann Kaiser. *Living Through Personal Crisis*. Chicago: The Thomas More Press, 1984.

Tilleraas, Perry. *The Color of Light: Hazelden Meditation Series*. Center City, MN: Hazelden Foundation, 1988.

Whitfield, Charles L. *Healing the Child Within: Discovery and Recovery for Adult Children of Dysfunctional Families*. Deerfield Beach, FL: Health Communications, Inc., 1987.

Wilkinson, Bruce. *The Prayer of Jabez: Breaking Through to the Blessed Life*. Sisters, OR: Multnomah Publishers, 2000.

Notes

[1]   Alcoholics Anonymous. *Alcoholics Anonymous*. (New York: AA World Services, Inc., Third Edition, 1976), 58.

[2]   Carolyn Osiek, *Beyond Anger*, Chapters 3 and 5.

[3]   Alcoholics Anonymous, 63.

[4]   Ibid., 64.

[5]   Ibid., 552.

[6]   Ibid., 76.

[7]   Perry Tilleraas, *The Color of Light* (Center City, MN: Hazelden Foundation, 1988), September 25.

[8]   Alcoholics Anonymous. *Alcoholics Anonymous*. (New York: AA World Services, Inc., Third Edition, 1976), 83-84.

Books by John Monbourquette

How to Love Again*
Moving from Grief to Growth

Are you suffering from a deep loss in your life? *How to Love Again* is a book that can offer you comfort in a time of despair. It is intended to accompany you on the journey you are about to make. You may want to read it from cover to cover, meditate on it, or refer back to those passages that most inspire you.

Author John Monbourquette describes the kind of healing that comes after loss: "In the same way the physical body deals with a physical wound, the emotional body begins a healing process the moment the emotional trauma occurs. Allow the natural wisdom of your healing system to come to your rescue. Eventually the pain will subside, and you will then be more aware of life around you, more open to happiness, more fully human once again.

"Throughout this journey, I would like you to face your pain and to recognize it peacefully. This attitude will help you survive. It will facilitate your healing process and will actually help you to benefit from your own suffering.

"In this way, you will move from grief to growth, and learn how to love again."

- 168 pages
- paperback

* Revised edition, previously published as *To Love Again: Finding Comfort and Meaning in Times of Grief.*

Books by John Monbourquette

How to Forgive
A Step-by-Step Guide

"What does it take to forgive?" asks John Monbourquette, best-selling author, psychologist and priest. His answer is a unique twelve-step guide which offers profound and practical advice on overcoming the emotional, spiritual and psychological blocks to true forgiveness.

Monbourquette begins by exploring the nature of forgiveness and exploding some of the myths. He shows how essential forgiveness is for us all, whatever our beliefs, for forgiveness touches on all aspects of the human person, the biological and psychological as well as the spiritual. He then takes the reader through his twelve-step healing process, providing practical exercises, case histories, anecdotes and even poetry along the way.

How to Forgive is an honest and touching book which unlocks the liberating and transformative power of forgiveness.

- 198 pages
- paperback

Books by John Monbourquette

How to Befriend Your Shadow
Welcoming Your Unloved Side

Each of us has a "shadow," composed of everything we have driven back into our unconscious for fear of being rejected by the people we loved when we were young. Over the years, we created a whole underground world filled with things that were shameful, displeasing or upsetting to those around us.

Our task as adults is to rediscover what makes up our shadow, to bring it into the light, and to use it for our own spiritual growth. If we refuse to do this work, we risk being out of balance psychologically, and our lives and relationships will not reach their fullest potential.

Is your shadow your friend or your enemy? That will depend on how you see it and how you relate to it. This book offers you the tools you need to welcome your shadow side. Befriend your shadow, and watch your relationship with yourself and with others grow and deepen!

- 160 pages
- paperback

Books by John Monbourquette

How to Discover Your Personal Mission
The Search for Meaning

What is your personal mission in life? Many of us find it hard to answer this question. It is so easy to get caught up in the day-to-day concerns of paying the rent and putting food on the table that we lose sight of the bigger picture. Whether we are young or not so young, we may feel that we haven't quite found our mission; that we're not doing what we feel we should be doing.

How to Discover Your Personal Mission invites you on an adventure to discover your personal mission. In this user-friendly book, best-selling author John Monbourquette will lead you through a three-stage process: learning to let go of the past; deepening your sense of identity and mission; and risking a new beginning in life. Through exercises and reflection, you will find the path that leads you in the direction that your soul is calling you. It may appear in the form of an ideal to pursue, a passion, a goal to strive for, or a deep and persistent desire.

Let the journey begin…

- 198 pages
- paperback

Books on Christian Meditation

Frequently Asked Questions
About Christian Meditation
The Path of Contemplative Prayer

Paul Harris

"Is meditation really prayer?" "How can I set aside an hour a day to meditate?" "What if I fall asleep during meditation?" "Does God speak to us in meditation?"

These are just a few of the 56 questions answered in this book, which is a compilation of answers to the most frequently asked questions posed to Paul Harris, a meditator who gives talks and workshops on Christian Meditation across North America and around the world. An honest, practical guide to the discipline of Christian Meditation, it offers encouragement, support and information that will help anyone interested in meditation – beginners and experienced meditators alike – on their contemplative journey.

- 240 pages
- paperback

Books on Christian Meditation

The Heart of Silence
Contemplative Prayer by Those Who Practise It

Paul Harris

In a world increasingly aware of the need for inner stillness, the 60 meditators in this book speak about a path of prayer that is anchored in both Christian tradition and contemplative experience, that is ever new: a path beyond words, thoughts and imagination into the presence of the risen Lord who dwells in our hearts in silence.

- 224 pages
- paperback

Christian Meditation
Contemplative Prayer for a New Generation

Paul Harris

Drawing on the teaching of Scripture and of Dom John Main, this book provides novices and experienced meditators alike with instruction and encouragement for the contemplative journey.

- paperback
- 146 pages

Books on Christian Meditation